Software Cost Estimation

Dr. KAPIL SHARMA

CreateSpace, Charleston SC, USA

ISBN-10: 1511410523
ISBN-13: 978-1511410526

DEDICATION

To my parents, Kamla Devi and Din Dayal.

CONTENTS

ACKNOWLEDGMENTS

The author's heartiest and deepest gratitude to almighty God whose grace provided him the perseverance, guidance, inspiration and strength to complete this book. He also wishes to express his thanks to all his friends (specially Juhi Jain), colleagues and other staff members who have directly or indirectly helped him during the completion of this book.

Last but not the least, the author expresses sincere thanks to his wife Manju Bala, who stoically and steadfastly shared her joys and sorrows and extended full support for this book. He cannot forget to keep on record the contribution of his daughters, Jiya & Ira who has been deprived of love and care for which they deserved.

ACKNOWLEDGMENTS

Chapter One: **Introduction**

1.1 Introduction to software cost estimation

Estimation of the cost estimation in software development remained the one the challenging problem even after the 40 years of the research. This estimation problem has already lead project managers, software engineers and analysts into the trouble for decades. The estimation of the cost and the schedule is based on determining the size of the system which is to be developed.

Initial estimate of the cost involves many uncertain elements. Early and reliable estimation is tuff task because it requires knowledge of many elements that are not known in the beginning or at the early stages. But early estimates are obviously mandatory for bidding of the contract. Also, determination of feasibility of the project in the terms of cost-benefit analysis also requires the early cost prediction. So, prediction will definitely guide decision making but it will be useful only when it is accurate. Many cost estimation models exist in literature. Many studies have been conducted for the evaluation of the models. Several researches showed that accuracy can be improved greatly if the model is calibrated to particular organization. Cost estimation relies on the some extent on the past experience also. So it is important need of the software industry to develop a model which is easy to use, calibrate and understand.

Effort estimation of software means, we want to know the amount of effort to be put in the development of software. It is usually measured by the number of person-hours that were spent in developing the software from specification until delivery. The prediction of the effort to be consumed in a software project is the most sought after variable in the process of project management as its determination in the early stages of a software project drives the planning of remaining activities.

It's been used as input to iteration plans, project plans ,budgets, pricing processes, investment analyses, bid proposals and deciding the execution boundaries of the project (Molokken, 2007). It's a critical activity for planning and monitoring software project development and for delivering the product on time and within budget.(Q. Alam)

It has been observed that most of the project goes out of the budget and also crosses their time limits since the prediction of the software effort before development is a critical issue. If managers are not able to accurately predict that how much manpower and time will be needed to fulfill the requirements of the project it may cause heavy loss to the organization. Because of this software effort estimation is one of the most challenging tasks of the project management.

Lots of research has been done in this field and so many models have been proposed and tested for the effort estimation but none of them is found suitable for all type of organization .Since each organization have its own parameters and capability and technology of development is also changing very rapidly that why predication may vary for the different organization. Bat algorithm is one of contemporary algorithm that's why it is able to adopt the current development environment and hence it is able to optimize the results better as compared to the tradition effort estimation models.

The advantages of this method are:

- It is one of the latest algorithm that's why it adopts better the latest development environment and technology.
- The technical team and mangers can factor define project parameters caused by new technologies and applications and languages as well involved in the project
- It can also cope with the exceptional personnel and characteristics, interactions as well.

1.1.1 Why is proper effort estimation important?

- Effort estimation is essential for many people and different departments in an organization as it is needed at various points of a project lifecycle.
- Presales teams need effort estimation in order to know the cost price of custom software. Without effort estimation pricing is impossible and the price you will give will probably bind you for the whole project, so it is important to have a good estimation from the beginning.
- Project managers need it in order to allocate resources and timely plan a project.
- In order to plan a project and inform the project owners about deadlines for submitting the project. It also shows if you have the resources to finish the project within customer or project owner predefined time limits, based on your available man power.

1.2 Cost estimation process (Mansor & Kasirun)

Cost estimation process is the prediction process to get the closest result with required cost. It involves the process of considering, experiences, time constraints, resources, risks, schedules, methods used, the required cost and other processes, which are related to development of a project. Hence, it is very important in managing a project particularly to the project manager, when he is proposing budget for certain project. In software development, there is widely used term known as "software project estimation", its function is to find the estimation process. Cost estimation, it is the calculation of quantity and prediction within a scope of the costs, which is required to develop and give a facility to manufacture goods and to furnish a service. These costs include an evaluation and assessments of uncertainties and risks. This process determines and considers utilized experience by an expert, forecasting and calculating the future cost of schedule, resources and methods for any project development. It supplies input to the original baselines and changes baselines against cost comparisons in whole project. It is done at a certain point that is based on the available information and at a certain time. Usually, it includes cost estimation summary, cost estimation details and basis of estimation which give type of cost estimation including risk, estimation methodologies, project details, cost adjustment and cost driven and so on. Estimation is depicted as "black art" due to its subjective behaviour. One person may take a day to complete a task, but another person can require just few hours to do same. Due to this when many people are asked to do estimation, they may give different answers as well as results. But if work is actually performed, actual amount of the time that is taken by the process is calculated and all the estimations that did not come close to that actual are considered inaccurate. If a person is not involved in estimation process, than estimations are just an attempt, to predict required resources and cost. It is very important to assume that, project will come in time, to improve accuracy of estimation process and have good estimation practices. Therefore, the project manager can help to develop a successful estimation for software project by understanding and applying good techniques, this makes estimation more accurate. Software project estimation is problem solving and in many cases; the problem which needs to be solved is very complex to be considered in single piece. For solving the problem, decompose it and restructure it to a smaller problem. Main purpose of software cost estimation is to lessen the amount of the predicted actual cost.

Software estimation is very important and any error in cost estimation can make a difference between loss and profit. All the factors must be considered and properly calculated. Over cost will results in bad impact to the company and to the developer. In actual life, cost estimation process is very difficult since it requires estimator to consider large number of factors and variables for example training costs, hardware costs, travel government policies costs, man power, environmental, effort, and expertise advices. Effort costs are usually least predictable and the largest development effort. Hence, most software cost estimations determines the effort cost using the unit man-month (MM). All of these factors will influence the overall effort and cost involved in any project that someone wants to develop. Therefore, one requires something that can provide better result in estimation to achieve the accurate result.

1.3 The Importance of Software Cost Estimation

The main motive of using software cost estimation by any organization is to fix when, whey and how cost estimation of any software is done. Cost estimation is important because:

- For proper planning purpose, for the purpose of approval and for finalizing the budget. In every company, it is the senior manager who takes the strategic decisions that are based on the accuracy of the estimation. Cost estimation also helps in deciding whether to take particular project. Also for ongoing project it helps to decide whether to continue with the ongoing project, delay the project or to stop the project.
- While the development of any software or any project, some sort of planning is required. Monitoring and control of implementation also need to be done by the project manager and the team leader. Again cost estimation is important for successful execution of all these tasks.
- Project Team Understanding: Cost estimation can be related to the work break down structure of the project. Each member is given certain task for estimation which is to be completed. (Mansor & Kasirun)
- For managing software projects in better way, the need of different resources should match completely with the different actual requirements.
- Software cost estimation should be done accurately because customer always expects the estimated cost should approx the actual cost.
- To improve the overall businesses plan so that all the resources may be used in efficient way.
- Accuracy of cost estimation process is also important for defining the resources required to verify, produce and validate different software products and for management of the various activities require for software development. It also helps in deciding if price of the tools is offset by improvement in productivity.
- Problem with the software cost estimation
- The main intrinsic problem that exists in the software cost estimation because of the inaccuracy of cost estimation models. Actually, different models fit for the different environments in which software are developed. Other factors that contributes in the inaccuracy of cost estimation are , imprecise and ambiguously stated requirements, lack of information on past and similar projects, and the models that developed for particular kind of data cannot be transferred easily to the other environments .
- Also, the Software projects vary over wide range, from the single

person project costing around few thousand dollars to the megaprojects that involves thousands of people and costs around hundreds of millions of dollars. Now, all tools and method must deal with this range. Obviously, a small and a big project will not have same estimation accuracy.

1.4 Introduction to Bacterial Foraging Optimization Algorithm

In the last forty years, researchers have been trying to simulate the biological systems from various aspects and proposed some effective bionic algorithms, including artificial neural network (ANN), genetic algorithm (GA), ant colony optimization (ACO), particle swarm optimization (PSO) and artificial immune system (AIS), etc. These bionic algorithms provide novel paradigms for engineering problems by mimic the specific structures or behaviours of certain creatures. (Wu, Zhang, Jiang, Jinhui, & Liang, 2007).Bacterial foraging optimization algorithm (BFOA) has been widely used and also accepted as a contemporary optimization algorithm of current interest for distributed optimization and control. BFOA is inspired by the social foraging behavior of *Escherichia coli*. BFOA has drawn the attention of researchers because of its good efficiency in solving the complex real-world optimization problems that are available in several application domains. The underlying biology behind the foraging strategy of *E.coli* is emulated in an extraordinary manner and used as a simple optimization algorithm. (Das, Biswas, Dasgupta, & Abraham, 2009).The Bacteria Foraging is bio inspired algorithm which estimates the cost function after each iterative step of the program as the program execution proceeds and leads to comparatively better fitness. The parameters that are to be optimized represent coordinates of the bacteria. Again the parameters are discredited in the required desirable range and each set of these discrete values represent a point in space coordinates. Then one bacterium is created and positioned at each point. After each progressive step the bacteria move to new positions and at each position cost function is calculated, then this calculated value of cost function and further movement of bacteria is decided by decreasing direction of cost function. After this the bacteria finally moves to a position (set of optimization parameters) with highest fitness value. The foraging strategy of E. Coli. The Bacteria is governed by four processes. These are swarming, chemotaxis, reproduction and dispersal elimination and. Chemotaxis is achieved by swimming and tumbling. When the bacterium meets favorable environment (rich in nutrients and noxious free), it continues swimming in the same direction. Decrease in cost function represents favorable environment, while increase in cost function represents unfavorable environment. When it meets unfavorable environment it tumbles (changes direction). By bringing mean square error to the minimal value the bacteria move out from their respective places in ring of cells.(Sharma, Pattnaik, & Garg, 2012).

1.5 Motivation

Though many cost estimation models are already developed in the literature but none of them is accurate to determine the software cost precisely. So, there is a need to determine the cost with little more accuracy. Also, models should be evaluated and ranked in the some way so as to find the most accurate model.

Software projects development can be considered to be the most uncertain and complex when compared to other types of engineering projects. The 2009 Standish Group Chaos report (The 10 laws of chaos, 2009) showed that only 32% of such projects succeeded and were delivered on time, with the required features and functions within budget: 44% did not meet these three requirements, and 24% failed, they were cancelled prior to completion. Based on the results of several investigations of software development projects, the main areas responsible for project failure were found to be as follows: project goal setting, improper project scheduling, ambiguous customer requirements, unmanaged risks, improper project execution, project staffing (availability and capabilities), stakeholder politics, and commercial pressures (Five reason why software projects fail, 2002).

Reason for all these failures can be weak project planning and management. For both we need proper effort estimation. When we get the requirements from customers, we need to tell the customer about pricing and time required for its completion. This is required as input to project plans, iteration plans, budgets, investment analyses, resource allocation scheme etc. Thus we can say that proper effort estimation is important from the starting point of project and till the end of it.

But over the past few years, software development effort is found to be one of the worst estimated attributes. Scientific studies show the poor state of software effort estimation. A recent review (M.jorgensen, 2003) reports that 70-80% of software development projects overrun their estimates and that average overruns are about 30-40%.Significant over or underestimation can be very expensive for company as Overestimation results in wasting of resources, whereas underestimation results in schedule/budget overruns and thus quality compromise. (F. Ferrucci, 2010)

The problem of accurate effort estimation is still open and the project manager is confronted at the beginning of the project with the same question that what effort is required for project (Dolado, 2009)

For support of project managers in a software development, several models have been developed to calculate the required Effort. The most significant effort estimation models that have been used in software development projects are:

- The Constructive Cost Model (COCOMO) (Boehm., 1981)
- The System Evaluation and Estimation of Resource Software Evaluation Model (SEER-SEM) (Segundo, 2001)
- Putnam Model (Putnam, 1978)
- Function Point Model (Albrecht, 1979)

COCOMO is still the good approach for some software projects. If you're using a traditional approach, with third generation language, such as C++ and development .The processes haven't changed much then COCOMO will give you good results. Companies generally use two to three methods for effort estimation and one of them is generally COCOMO. (Facts about COCOMO And Costar, 2012) Thus we can say that COCOMO model is the most widely used estimation model for software project.

Further to solve the problem of accurate effort estimation many optimization algorithms such as particle swarm optimization, genetic algorithm, firefly algorithm, cuckoo search algorithm, Bat Algorithm etc. have been incorporated with these models to further improve them. (Brajesh Kumar Singh, 2013), (sheta, 2006) (Reddy, 2010) (Sheta, 2007) (P.R Srivastava, 2014)

Here we propose a new calibrated Intermediate COCOMO model (for all types of system i.e. Organic, semi-detached and embedded) with Bat Algorithm, where we have calculated new values for coefficients a and b. For calculation we have used the dataset of NASA 63 projects. Results show that optimized COCOMO model with Bat Algorithm give more better results in terms of MMRE of all projects.

1.6 Book Objective

With the motivation explained in the previous section and the objective can be identified as:

- To find the parameters of COCOMO model and four of its variants using BFOA algorithm, this has already proven its effectiveness in other engineering domains.
- To evaluate all the models using 17 comparison criteria.
- To find the best of the five model using DBA theory.
- To develop New calibrated COCOMO model with Bat Algorithm.
- To do in deep study of Bat Algorithm and map BAT Algorithm to COCOMO Model.
- To develop calibrated model for all organic, semidetached and embedded systems in Intermediate model of COCOMO.
- Compare the result of original Intermediate COCOMO Model with newly calibrated model in terms of MMRE (Mean Magnitude of Relative Error).

- Much more calibrated with the company environment and past experience.
- Quantification of the experience factor.

1.7 Main contents of Book.

The book is organized as follows:

Chapter 2: Soft computing and effort estimation

This chapter discusses different techniques used to estimate the cost of the software. For example, estimation with the help of neural networks, genetic algorithm, and particle swarm optimization. It also discusses different modifications of the bacterial foraging optimization algorithm like improved BFO, hybrid BFO, self- adapting BFO. Apart from all this some of the applications of the BFO are also discussed.

Chapter 3: Bacterial Foraging Optimization Algorithm

This chapter discussed the bacterial foraging optimization algorithm in detail. The main constituent steps of the algorithm i.e. chemotaxis, reproduction, swarming, and elimination dispersal are highlighted. Apart from this influence of various parameters used in the algorithm are discussed.

Chapter 4: Software Cost Estimation

This chapter mainly discusses the COCOMO model and its types. Some of the variations of the model whose parameters are evaluated using bacterial foraging optimization algorithm are also discussed. Least square is also discussed.

Chapter 5: BAT Optimization

This Chapter explain bat optimization algorithm for COCOMO.

Chapter 6 : Distance Based Approach

This chapter explains the theory DBA. The theory was applied in order to select the most appropriate model. Some criteria are discussed based on which models will be evaluated.

Chapter 7: Cost estimation using BAFO

Software Cost estimation models have been implemented and ranked based on Matlab scripting language

Chapter 8: Optimized cocomo model with bat algorithm.

This chapter finally gives the proposed approach and the results obtained. The parameters of COCOMO and some of its modifications are determined with the help of bacterial foraging optimization algorithm. Finally all the models are evaluated against certain criteria. These criteria are used by DBA to determine the best model.

Chapter Two: **Soft computing and effort estimation**

2.1 Introduction to software cost estimation

Software cost estimation is the process by which cost to develop the software can be determined before it has been developed actually. It helps to plan and track the process of software development. Controlling the investment in the software development is one of the important steps in software project management. Making accurate software cost estimate is still one of the challenging tasks before the industry. Estimation is helpful when it is made at the early stage when the project is approved. However, estimating the values at the early stages is difficult. Since the cost estimation process is the crucial part in any development process.

2.2 An overview with the evolution of effort estimation techniques

Software development effort estimation is the process of predicting the effort required to develop or maintain software based on uncertain, incomplete and noisy input, past experience and data. Effort estimates may be used by the managers as input to budgets, project plans and investment analyses, pricing processes etc.

2.2.1 Who should do effort estimation and who is interested in it?

Usually Project Managers are responsible for effort estimation. Depending on the chosen effort estimation method, they can estimate alone or with expert advice from developers, designers and testers.

Apart from managers, project owners and sales people need most of the effort estimation. Most of the times, your effort estimation may be challenged by sales or management teams. There exists a bridge between sales people and developer's team regarding efforts as Sales people want low cost whereas developers and designers know the actual time and resources required for development. Thus when giving estimates, they will take the worst case scenario.

2.3 Estimation approaches

Estimation Approaches can be categorized as (Shepperd, 2007):

- **Expert estimation:** It's based on judgment process by the experts. The quantification step is the step where the estimate produced is based on past experience of the experts.
- **Formal estimation model:** The quantification step is based on physical processes, e.g., the use of a formula that is derived from historical data.
- **Combination-based estimation:** The quantification step is based on mechanical and judgmental combinations of estimates from different

sources.

In Table 2.1 classifications of estimation approaches within each category is illustrated:

Table 2.1: Categorization of Estimation Approaches

Estimation approach	Category	Examples
Analogy-based estimation	Formal estimation model	ANGEL
WBS-based (bottom up) estimation	Expert estimation	company specific activity templates
Parametric models	Formal estimation model	COCOMO, SLIM, SEER-SEM
Size-based models	Formal estimation model	Function Point Analysis, Use Case Analysis
Group estimation	Expert estimation	Planning poker, Wideband Delphi
Mechanical combination	Combination-based estimation	Average of an analogy-based and a Work breakdown structure-based effort estimate
Judgmental combination	Combination-based estimation	Expert judgment based on estimates from a parametric model and group estimation

2.4 Expert estimation

2.4.1 Expert Judgment Method:

In this technique we consult with software cost estimation expert or a nexus of the experts to use their industrial experience and analysis of the proposed project to arrive at maximal estimate of its cost. A group consensus technique or Delphi technique is the most efficient way to be used.

The estimation steps used in this method:

- Coordinators present each and every expert with a specification and an approximate estimation form.
- Coordinator calls a group meeting in which the discussion with the experts for estimation issues with each.
- All Experts have to fill the forms anonymously
- Coordinator release and distributes a brief summary of the estimation on an iteration form.
- A group meeting is called by coordinator and experts are invited to discuss their points and estimates with variety of ideas.
- Again all Experts fill forms anonymously; steps 4 and 6 are iterated for

appropriate number of rounds.

The advantages of this method are:

- Differences between past project experience and requirements of the new proposed project can be intimated by experts.
- The experts can suggest about the impacts that might be caused by new technologies, applications and languages that are involved in the future project and can also a good factor in exceptional personnel characteristics interactions and formulizations.

The disadvantages include:

This is not feasible to quantify this method as it is hard to document the factors used by the experts or group of experts.

2.5 Formal estimation models

2.5.1 Estimating by Analogy

Here comparisons are made between the previously proposed projects and the new methodology presented here where the project development information id known. The proposed project has been estimated by extrapolation of actual data from the completed project. This method can be used at both either at component-level or at the system-level. Estimation by analogy is comparatively more straightforward, and in some respects it is formal and systematic form of judgment from experts.

The steps used in estimation by analogy are:

- Characterization of the proposed project.
- Selecting the similar type of projects that are already completed and the characteristics have been stored in the data repositories.
- Analyzing the estimates of the proposed project from the similar completed projects.

The main advantages of this method are:

- Estimation is based characteristics of actual project data.
- Past knowledge and experience of the estimator's might be used that is not easy to quantify.
- The relative differences between the already completed and proposed project can be identified and impacts have to be estimated by the experts.

Top-Down Estimating Method

Top-down estimation methodology is also known as Macro Model. In the top-down estimation method, an overall cost estimation for the project is calculated from the global properties of the project, and afterwards the project is partitioned into many low-level components. This methodology is having tremendous scope in early cost estimation where only global properties are known. It is quite useful in the early phases of the software development since sufficient information not available.

The advantages of this method are:

- System-level activities are mainly focused for example documentation, integration, and configuration management. Many of them are generally ignored in other similar methods and it does not leave out the cost of system-level functions of the project under consideration.
- Minimal project details are required which makes it faster and easier to implement.

The disadvantages are:

- Low level problems are generally not identified and are likely to escalate costs.
- No detailed basis for justifying decisions or estimates is achieved yet.

The leading method using this approach is Putnam model.

Putnam model:

Another popular software cost model is the Putnam model. The form of this model is:

Technical constant C= size * B $^{1/3}$ * T $^{4/3}$

Total Person Months B=1/T ^{4} *(size/C) ^{3}

T= Required Development Time in years

Size is estimated in Lines of code Where: C is a parameter dependent on the development environment and it is determined on the basis of historical data of the past projects.

Rating: C=2,000 (poor), C=8000 (good) C=12,000 (excellent)

Function Point Analysis

The function point measurement method was developed by Allan Albrecht at IBM. (Albrecht, 1979) The Function Point Analysis is another method of quantifying the size and complexity of a software system in terms of the functionalities that user has demanded. Albrecht believes function points offer several significant advantages over SLOC counts of size measurement.

There are two steps in counting function points:

- **Count of the user functions:** The raw function counts are derived by considering a linear combination of five commonly known software components: external outputs external inputs, logic internal files, external inquiries, and external interfaces. There are three complexity levels: complex, average and simple. There after the sum of these numbers are weighted according to prior calculated complexity level, which is known as the number of function counts (FC).
- **Adjustment of environmental processing complexity:** The final function point are calculated by multiplying FC by the adjustment factor which is determined by considering 14 factors of processing complexity. FC is modified by at most 35%.

Following are the two primary motivations for function point data collection:

1). Desire by managers to monitor levels of productivity.
2) Estimation of software development cost.

Bottom-up Estimation Method

Using bottom-up estimation method, the cost of each and every software components is estimated and henceforth the results are combined to reach at an estimated cost of overall project. The final aim is construction of overall estimate of a system from the knowledge accumulated about the small software components and their interactions.

The advantages:

- It allows the software managers to handle an estimate the cost in traditional method.
- It is relatively more stable because the estimation of errors in the various components can be balanced out.

The disadvantages:

- Many system level costs might be overlooked that are associated with software development.
- It can be inaccurate sometimes because the complete information may not be available in the early phases of software development.

The leading method using this approach is COCOMO model.

(C.F, 1996)Performed an empirical validation of four algorithmic models (SLIM, COCOMO, Estimates and FPA) using data from projects outside the original model development environments without re-calibrating the models. The results indicate to what extent these models are generalizable to different environments. Most models showed a strong over-estimation bias and large estimation errors with the mean absolute relative error (MARE) ranging from an average of 57 percent to almost 800 percent. Thus we can combine these models with non-algorithmic models such as (PSO, Genetic Algorithm, Fuzzy Logic, Neural Network) (S K Sehra, 2011) and get better results.

While doing this work, we have gone through some literature where non algorithmic models are used with COCOMO model, which can be shown as:

He (Basili, 1981) presented a model process which permits the development of effort estimation model for any particular organization. The model is based on data collected by that organization which captures its particular environment factors and differences in its particular projects. The process provides capability for producing a model tailored to the organization which can be more effective than any model originally developed for other environment. They demonstrated it using data collected for the Software Engineering laboratory at NASA and came to conclusion that

Effort= $a(\text{size in KLOC})^{b} + c * (\text{methodology})$

Sheta (sheta, 2006) presented two new model structures to estimate the effort required for the development of software projects using Genetic

Algorithms (GAs). A modified version of the famous COCOMO model provided to explore the effect of the software development adopted methodology in effort computation. The performances of the developed models were tested on NASA software project dataset. The developed models were able to provide good estimation capabilities.

Anish et. al. (Anish M, Kamal P and Harish M, 2010) presented two new models, based on fuzzy logic. Rather than using a single number, the software size is regarded as a triangular fuzzy number. We can optimize the estimated effort for any application by varying arbitrary constants for these models. The developed models were tested on 10 NASA software projects, on the basis of four criterions for assessment of software cost estimation models. Comparison of all the models was done and it is found that the developed models provide better estimation.

Reddy (Reddy, 2010)Proposed three software effort estimation models by using soft computing techniques: Particle Swarm Optimization with inertia weight for tuning effort parameters in COCOMO Model. The performance of the developed models was tested by NASA software project dataset provided by (Basili, 1981). The developed models were able to provide good estimation capabilities.

Sheta (Sheta, 2007) proposed Differential Evolution (DE) as an alternative technique and powerful tool to estimate the COCOMO model parameters. The performances of the developed models were tested on NASA software project dataset provided by (Basili, 1981). The developed COCOMO-DE model was able to provide good estimation capabilities.

Lin (Lin J.-C. , 2010) used Pearson product moment correlation coefficient to select several factors then used K-Means clustering algorithm to software project clustering. After project clustering, he use Particle Swarm Optimization that take mean of MRE (MMRE) as a fitness value and N-1 test method to optimization of COCOMO parameters.

Anna et. al. (Anna Galinina, Olga Burceva, Sergei Parshutin, 2012) used Genetic algorithm to optimize COCOMO model coefficients which were determined in 1981 by means of the regression analysis of statistical data based on 63 different types of project data. The proposed algorithm was tested and the obtained results were compared with the ones obtained using the current COCOMO model coefficients. Coefficients optimized by the GA in the organic mode produces better results in comparison with the results obtained using the current COCOMO model coefficients.

Vishali et. al. (Vishali, Anshu Sharma, Suchika Malik, 2014)used Genetic algorithm and Ant Colony Optimization to optimize COCOMO model coefficients which were determined in 1981 by means of the regression analysis of statistical data based on 63 different types of project data. Results were better for GA and ACO as compared to normal COCOMO Model.

Software cost estimation using neural network

Attarzadeh et.al. (Attarzadeh & Ow, 2010) proposed COCOMO using the soft computing approach with some of the desirable features of neural networks approach like good interpretability and learning ability were used to develop the model. The model proposed could be validated and interpreted by the experts. They also had good generalization capacity in contrast to the other neural models. The reliability of the estimation was enhanced since the model dealt with uncertain and imprecise input data as well. Software effort drivers that were used for calculating software effort was generally observed to have two properties vagueness and uncertainty. But using neural network in software effort estimation model had overcome these characteristics. But still for reliable and accurate estimation choice of appropriate neural network played an important role. Neural Networks played better role than other techniques with some of the test cases. Neural network was applied to both algorithmic and non-algorithmic model and it was proved that more accurate estimates were produced. The proposed neural networks model showed better software effort estimates in view of the MMRE, Pred(0.25) evaluation criteria as compared to the traditional COCOMO(Attarzadeh & Ow, 2010). Neural Network produced better results than COCOMO.

Kotb et.al.(Kotb, Haddara, & Ko, 2011) surveyed that majority of times effort is estimated by family of COCOMO model. Kotb et.al.was focused basically to replace the COCOMO model with other model that can be used easily with ERP adoptions. Cost was estimated using neural networks and training algorithm used was back propagation feed forward. Finally results of the model as well as its advantages and shortcomings of the model were also discussed. The model was initially used for small and medium sized enterprises but it can be expanded to other environments and contexts. The model was proposed to minimize the role of project managers and other concerned person to define various parameters like function points for giving as input. Since the proposed framework was based on neural network, hence a training algorithm was required to be chosen. So, feed forward back-propagation algorithm was used. Neural network generally has 3 layers and those are input layer, hidden layer and the output layer. Number of neurons in the input layer was kept equal to the number of data factors. Number of neurons in the middle layer was kept equal to the number of neuron in the input layer. Finally thirty six output neurons were kept in the output layer which covers wide range of cost from thousands to billions. BCD encoding was used, so that every digit was represented by the four neurons. For successful and accurate cost estimation data was required to be collected accurately. It was one of the key factors for successful estimation. So, inappropriate data was thrown away in starting itself. Other factor for unsuccessful estimation was noise.

The accuracy of the model was limited by noise present.
Attarzadeh et.al. (Attarzadeh & Ow, 2010) proposed two models. First model was an artificial neural network model that supplements COCOCMO model to determine the cost of software at early stages itself. ANN-COCOMO II model was the second model proposed. The suggested models used advantages of both artificial neural network like good interpretability and learning and COCOMO model. To determine the attributes from the past projects neural network was used. For evaluation of models 156 sets of project data from COCOMO I and NASA93 were used. The analysis of the obtained results shows 8.36% improvement in estimation accuracy in the ANN-COCOMOII model, when compared with the original COCOMO II(Attarzadeh, Mehranzadeh, & Barati, 2012). MMRE was used for evaluation of the results obtained.

In (Kaushik, Chauhan, Mittal, & Gupta, 2012) paper, most widely used software cost estimation model the Constructive Cost Model (COCOMO) was discussed. The model was implemented using artificial neural networks. In addition to this it was trained using one of the learning algorithm. Here, perceptron learning algorithm was used. COCOMO data set was used for the purpose of training and testing the overall network. The results obtained were compared with that of the actual results from the COCOMO model. The overall aim of the research was to increase the accuracy of the results that were obtained by COCOMO by the introduction of the neural network. The idea basically was to form the model that will map COCOMO model to neural network with minimum number of layers and minimum number of nodes so as to increase performance of network. It was concluded that by the use of artificial neural network algorithm for modeling the COCOMO algorithm is one of an efficient way of accurate estimation. Values provided were nearly accurate.

Kaushik et.al.(Kaushik, Soni, & Soni, 2012)also used neural network for cost estimation. Neural network was applied on the well known COCOMO model. Again back propagation algorithm was used for training purpose. Two data sets were used for the testing purpose.

Cost estimation using PSO and Neural Network

Hari et.al.(Hari & Sethi, 2011) proposed Clustering-PSO-Neural Networks (CPN) based on Particle Swarm Optimization Algorithm for determining the parameters of COCOMO model. The technique was operated on data sets clustered by using K means clustering algorithm. Both clusters and parameters of the effort model were trained by using Neural Network for data classification. Training algorithm used was Back Propagation algorithm. The model was finally tested on COCOMO81 dataset. It was also compared with the standard model. By exploiting the experience of Neural Network and as well as parameter tuning property of PSO the proposed model was able to generate better results. The CPN model that was proposed was successfully applied on the large data sets. PSO generally gave better results when data set contains such projects which belong to similar genres.

Benala et.al (Benala, Chinnababu, Mall, & Dehuri, 2013) were concerned with cost estimation models that were based on Particle swarm optimized Functional link artificial neural networks (PSO-FLANN). PSO-FLANN, is a typical three layer feed forward neural network which consists of input layer, hidden layer and output layer. However in FLANN, the weight vector was evolved by PSO during training of the network. The FLANN architecture for predicting software development effort was a single-layer feed forward neural network consisting of one input layer and an output layer. The FLANN generated the output (effort) by expanding the initial inputs (cost drivers) and then processing in the final output layer. Each input neuron corresponded to a component of an input vector. The output layer consisted of one output neuron that computes the software development effort as a linear weighted sum of the outputs of the input layer. The large and non-normal data sets leaded FLANN methods to low prediction accuracy and high computational complexity. (Benala, Chinnababu, Mall, & Dehuri, 2013). So, the research was done in software cost estimation by using the hybridization of FLANN with PSO. It was also suggested that it can be extended further by using various other algorithms like ant colony optimization (ABC), Artificial Immune System (AIS), Annealing and fuzzy logic etc. Performance of PSO-FLANN was also evaluated. It provided better accuracy than that given by FLANN. Experimental results showed that method gave better accuracy in comparison to techniques like Step wise regression (SWR), classification and regression trees (CART) etc.

Cost estimation using Genetic Algorithm

For the purpose of estimation of effort two new models were introduced by Sheta et.al. (Sheta A. F., 2006). COCOMO model estimates the effort as a function of Developed Line of Code (DLOC). Two new models which were modifications of COCOMO model were introduced and they used additional parameter ME (methodology) adopted as input. Genetic Algorithm was used to determine various parameters used in the model. The models were used for computing the effort required for the project data set from NASA. The parameters which were estimated generalized the computation required for the calculation of effort. The performances of these models were tested on project dataset of NASA. Variance-Accounted-For (VAF) was finally used to check the performance.

Cost estimation using Simulated Annealing Algorithm

Multivariate interpolation models were proposed to estimate effort or cost required in software project. Effort function was represented by COCOMO based equation and data set consisted of two variables LOC

(Line of Code) and another one was ME (methodology) used. Simulated Annealing (SA) used in effort estimation is another heuristic approach to determine the parameters of COCOMO models. Simulated Annealing is commonly used method employed to compute the parameters of proposed models by applying an analogy between the way in which a metal cools and freezes becomes a crystalline structure of minimum energy and the search for a minimum in a more general system, the solution randomly walked in its neighborhood with a probability determined by Metropolis principle while the system temperature decreases slowly; when the annealing temperature was closing zero, the solution stayed at the global best solution in a high probability.(Uysal, 2008).

Factors that influences software cost estimation

Mansor et.al.(Mansor, Yahya, & Hj Arshad, 2011) intended to find out the factors that influences the cost estimation in software development. A conceptual model was developed from the review which showed the influence of various factors in cost estimation. These factors could help the software developers to estimate the cost with bit more accuracy. Five important factors in 1994 were reported by Standish CHOAS that were important in cost estimation process in software development. The factors were clearly stated requirements, involvement of user, executive management support, entertainment, realistic expectations and obviously proper planning. Role of project manager also cannot be overlooked. Some other factors that were considered were choosing appropriate methodology, choosing appropriate estimation technique, choice of appropriate tools, policies of the company, sponsors role. It was concluded that cost estimation in software development process can be improved if these factors were considered properly.

Realizing the fact that there are many dynamic and precarious attributes that are attached to each and every software project, the accuracy in the prediction of the cost will rely greatly on the prudential treatment of all of these attributes. Kashyap et.al.(Kashyap a & Misra, 2014) dealt with the methods of quantification, selection and comparison of various attributes related to various projects. Author had tried to find out similarity difference between various project attributes and then consequently used these differences measurement for creating an initial cost proposal of any software project that may had some degree of similarity or correspondence with the already completed projects and whose total cost is fairly established as well as well known. So, a method based on the 'similarity difference measure' for estimating the cost of software project. For calculating similarity difference between various softwares author had defined each software on the basis of three aspects, which were Linguistic Attributes, Nominal Attributes and Numerical Attributes. Author had described various methods so as to calculate similarity difference for each of the category. Then author had used these differences to find out the k most similar projects or to find out the nearest neighbours in similarity difference space. Author had also tried to validate the given procedure by using MMRE benchmark for measuring error.

Software cost estimation using fuzzy logic

Kumar and Rao proposed a fuzzy model for software cost estimation that handles obscurity and ambiguity. MATLAB was used for determining the parameters in various cost estimation models. The performance of model was evaluated on published software projects data. Various models for which parameters were determined were COCOMO basic model, COCOMO Inter(NOM), Detailed(NOM), Early Design Model(high), post Arch Model(H-H),Doty, Mittal model, Swarup model .Comparison of results from this model with existing ubiquitous models was done. Fuzzy logic was used to estimate the cost and MARE was used as for evaluating the performance. (Kumar & Rao, 2011).

Software cost estimation using fuzzy logic and PSO

To control the uncertainty in the effort estimation (Reddy & Hari, 2011) fuzzy logic along with parameters tuned by PSO (Particle Swarm Optimization) was used. Three models were proposed for the cost estimation by using PSO with Inertia weight and fuzzy logic. The estimated efforts were optimized with the use of incumbent archetypal and tested on data from NASA software. All models were compared against each other. Incumbent Archetypal was found to have better values. Models were proved best on the basis of VAF, MARE, and VARE.

Cost estimation based on Quality Assurance Coverage

Azath et.al. (Azath & Wahidabanu, 2012) proposed an efficient effort estimation system based on quality assurance coverage as estimation of software cost accurately is very big issue. The existing models did not give accurate results since they consider very few factors for estimating the cost. The work is the basis for the improvement in in the research of software effort estimation with a series of quality attributes along with constructive cost model (COCOMO). The further classification of software system for which approximate effort estimation has to be calculated is generally based on Constructive cost estimation model i.e. COCOMO classes. Quality assurance ISO 9126 quality factors were used and function point metrics is used as weighing factor for estimation. Effort are estimated for MS word 2007 using the following models: Albrecht and Gaffney model, Kemerer model, SMPEEM model and FP Matson, Barnettand Mellichamp model. In the proposed method, software effort was effectively estimated by using Function Points. The main differences between the proposed and contemporary estimation of effort for the software system development was the level of quality liberation, that is, the effort was estimated by using the minimum number of quality factors in existing methods, but in the proposed effort estimation method covers the ISO9126 quality factors, which was automatically reflected in the development of software. The main advantage of the proposed effort estimation system is that it manages imprecision and uncertainty correctly in the software project. It has been observed from the implementation results that the proposed method is effectively estimating efforts of the software project models.(Azath & Wahidabanu, 2012).

Software cost estimation using PSO

It is known that basic input for software cost estimation is the line of code i.e. coding size and also the set of cost drivers, and the output is Effort which is described in terms of Person-Months (PM's). In this paper, (Rao, Krishna, & Rao, 2014) author had proposed a model for determining the parameters of COCOMO model used in Software Cost Estimation with the help of MOPSO i.e. Multi Objective Particle Swarm Optimization. Parameters of the model were tuned by using MOPSO side by side considering two main objectives and those were Prediction and Mean Absolute Relative Error. Dataset COCOMO was considered to test the model. It was observed that the proposed model gave better results in comparison to the standard COCOMO model. It was also observed that providing enough classification of training data gave better result. Accuracy of cost estimation model was measured in the terms of its error rate. New model was proposed for estimation of software cost. To tune the parameters MOPSO methodology was applied. It was observed that MOPSO gave better results. When the performance of the model was tested in terms of the Prediction and MARE results were found useful. It was also noticed that the non-linearity in the used data items was being considered during the work for the testing and training tuning parameters and best way for bringing in some amount of linearity among these data items was by using clustering techniques. By the use of clustering method divide the data items which may be divided into a number of clusters and the PSO was then used for tuning of parameter of each cluster. The clusters and the tuned parameters were then trained by using the Neural Networks and efficient back propagation algorithms.

Software cost estimation using other methods

Mansor et.al.(Mansor & Kasirun) did a survey result of which concluded that two methods were used most commonly for software cost estimation. One of them was expert judgment. Expert judgment was based on the experience of the estimator and the past estimation histories. Other method that was used most prominently was based on COCOMO II. COMOCO II was said to provide good results since it took number of variables into consideration. So, it was suggested to use hybridization of both the models. Integration of both was suggested to be helpful for accurate estimation.

COCOMO was developed by Boehm which came under the category of algorithmic software cost estimation model. The model had increasingly three different forms and these are basic, intermediate and detailed. Basic COCOMO was suitable for quick, early and the rough order of estimated required in production of software but from accuracy point of view it was not very efficient. Intermediate COCOMO considers the project attributes also. So, it was bit more efficient than basic. In detailed COCOMO in addition to all this phase of project is also considered. COCOMO technique is in use since 1981. After that some of the intelligent techniques were introduced so as to obtain results more accurately. Some of the data mining techniques were introduced and results of these were compared to the standard results obtained. Some of the techniques that were used was ANN, LR, K-NN and SVR. NASA's projects data were used for the purpose of training as well as testing. Finally the results obtained of data mining and COCOMO were compared (Khalifelua & Ghar, 2012). These data mining techniques were found to produce better results than the COCOMO model.

Satapathy et.al.(Satapathy, Kumar, & Rath, 2013)estimated the cost of various software projects using class point approach and optimize the parameters using six types of adaptive regression techniques such as multi-layer perceptron, multivariate adaptive regression splines (MRS), projection pursuit regression, constrained topological mapping, K nearest neighbour regression and radial basis function network to achieve better accuracy. Further, a comparative analysis of software effort estimation using these adaptive regression techniques had been provided. By estimating the effort required to develop software projects accurately, softwares with acceptable quality within budget and on planned schedules were expected. Finally the generated minimum results of different techniques had been compared to estimate their performance accuracy. Result showed that MRS based effort estimation model gave less value of NRMSE, MMRE and higher value of prediction accuracy. Hence it was concluded that the effort estimation using MRS model will provide more accurate results than other five techniques. The computations for above procedure had been implemented and membership functions generated using MATLAB.(Satapathy, Kumar, & Rath, 2013).

Lu et.al.(Lu & Yin, 2013) proposed the new model for testing project. The model given was named as Constructive Cost Model for Software Testing (CCMST). It contains the drivers used for software testing. The driver introduced was more complete then the previous models. Case study was used to prove validity and usability of model. Some, rating levels were also introduced by the CCMST model. It improved cost estimation by using cost drivers towards which researchers were not paying attention.

Sheta et. al. (Sheta & Aljahdali, 2013) **p**resented two new models for the purpose of effort estimation with the use of fuzzy logic. One of the models was proposed on the famous COCOMO model and it used source line of code as input to estimate the effort required. While the second model that was used takes Outputs, Inputs, User Inquiries and Files as input so as to estimate the FP (Function Point). The proposed model was reported for showing better results. Results were validated against the Albrecht data set.

Benala et.al.(Benala, Mall, Srikavya, & HariPriya, 2014) described the empirical study undertaken for investigating the quantitative aspect of application of data mining techniques in model building for purpose of Software effort estimation. Some example of techniques that were chosen are Logistic regression, Multi linear regression and CART. Empirical evaluation was carried out. That used three fold cross validation procedures which had been carried out with the use of three datasets of software projects, which were, Cocomo81, Nasa93, and Bailey Basili. It was observed that: (1) CART technique was suitable for Nasa93 and Nasa93_5. (2). Multiple Linear Regression was suitable for Nasa93_2, Cocomo81o, Cocomo81s, and Basili Bailey. (3). Logistic Regression was suitable for Cocomo81, Nasa93_1 and Cocomo81e. It was concluded that data mining techniques gave better results for unlimited data.

2.6 Introduction to Bacterial Foraging Optimization Algorithm

Biologically inspired algorithms mimic behavior of animals that they exhibit in some sort of group activity like foraging. Particle Swarm Optimization (PSO), Ant Colony Optimization (ACO), Artificial Bee Colony Optimization (ABC) are some of the algorithms developed on this ground. Bacterial Foraging Optimization Algorithm (BFOA) was given by Passino (Passino K. M., 2002). It has been used widely in many of the engineering problem related to optimization example harmonic estimation (Mishra, 2005), Parameter estimation of Wiener model (Huang & Lin, 2010), Assembly line problem (Atasagun & Kara, 2013), Autonomous Robot Path Planning (Hossain & Ferdous, 2014).

Bacterial Foraging Optimization Algorithm was developed to mimic the foraging strategy of Escherichia Coli Bacteria. E.coli is the rod shaped bacteria i.e. found in lower intestine of warm blooded organisms. E.coli always tries to move to place which has highest amount of nutrition and it avoids the harmful environment. Foraging is the process by which bacteria locate and ingest their food. Following are the integral part of E.coli bacterium i.e plasma membrane, cell wall, and capsule that contains the cytoplasm and nucleoid. The pili are used for a type of gene transfer to other E.coli bacterium, and flagellum is used for locomotion. The cell is about 2μm in length and 1 μm in diameter. The E.coli cell only weighs about 1 picogram and is about 70% water. Salmonella typhimurium is a similar type of bacterium.(Passino K. M., 2002) In suitable environment whenever E.coli gets longer it splits into two parts. For example on getting sufficient food and temperature of around 37 degree centigrade, it can develop everything it needs to replicate within 20 minutes. Hence in short time population can be doubled easily. It also has some sort of system that guides its search of food and help avoiding noxious environment. It will swim from noxious environment to healthy environment with the help of this control system.

If we map this to optimization problem then bacteria will have to move to position of highest nutrient value and this position will be optimum position. Bacteria can initially be placed at any of the random positions in the search space. Bacteria will move in the search space in order to find the optimum value. Process by which bacterium moves from one position to another position in order to find position with highest nutrient value in foraging is known as chemotaxis. This step simulates the movement of bacteria in the search space. Bacteria exhibit two operations while chemotaxis namely swimming and tumbling. Bacteria may perform swim followed by tumble or tumble followed by swim or tumble followed by tumble or it swims continuously depending on the medium in which it is searching for food. Bacterium uses flagella for swimming and tumbling. In each chemotactic step bacterium gets energy. Each bacterium undergoes certain fixed number of chemotactic steps. Amount of movement in particular direction is quantified by a parameter know as step size $c(i)$ where i is the bacterium under consideration. If value of $c(i)$ is kept large then algorithm may jump over the optimum point and if value of $c(i)$ is small then algorithm may take large time to converge.

After this health (sum of energy obtained at each chemotactic step) of each bacterium is calculated and bacteria are sorted according to the health. So bacteria in nutrient medium tend to reproduce and bacteria with poor nutrients tend to die. So half of the bacteria which are healthy reproduce on finding suitable conditions into two and the remaining half with poor health are eliminated. So, theory of natural selection is applicable here.

Finally, sometimes due to occurrence of some rare event like sudden rise in temperature or other, some or all bacteria may be migrated to other media.

2.7 Applications of Bacterial Foraging Optimization Algorithm

2.7.1 Application in Assembly Line Problem

Bacterial foraging optimization problem had been applied to assembly line balancing (ALB). In Assembly line balancing tasks are needed to be assigned to workstations (Atasagun & Kara, 2013). This is done so as to satisfy the precedence relations between cycle time and tasks restrictions while optimizing the performance. Entire production system is greatly affected by performance given by assembly lines. It is last stage of processes but has an important impact. So, obtaining effective solution in reasonable time for ALB problems is important. Problem by nature is NP Hard, so finding deterministic solution which gives result in polynomial time is quite tuff. However various heuristic and meta-heuristic solutions had already been suggested in literature for solving various simply straight and assembly line problems which are U-shaped. BFOA was one of the meta-heuristic approaches applied to this problem using well known data set. It was applied to both simple and U shaped problem. Number of tasks varied from 7 to 111 in data set. 128 test-problems were used and BFOA gave optimal solution for 123 test-problems within seconds. Since BFOA had shown quite competitive performance here, so it was expected that it can be applied to various other versions of ALB problems. BFOA can be hybridized with other meta-heuristic approaches or chemotactic step in the original BFOA can be modified to apply it on other complex version of the ALB problem.

2.7.2 Application in Autonomous Robot Path Planning in Dynamic Environment

A robot is reprogrammable and multifunctional intelligent device. It is intelligent because it can decide the actions it has to take depending on the environment. In case of mobile robot, path planning is one of the challenging tasks especially in dynamic environment where any random obstacle can occur. In static environment all the objects are static i.e. position remains fixed with time. However in dynamic environment objects are dynamic in nature means there position can change with time. They can move in different directions. The basic goal is to move robot from one point to another point through shortest possible path considering all the obstacles that occur in between i.e. to find the optimal path. Optimal path is the path which is better in terms of time, cost, energy, distance etc. But each of them has weakness associated with them. Than came various meta-heuristic techniques like PSO, ABC etc to solve the above problem. BFOA was used to solve this problem of moving robot continuously from current position to target position and avoiding obstacles side by side. Bacteria were considered to be distributed around the robot in a circle in a random fashion. Best bacterium was evaluated by finding distance to the target point and by using the Gaussian cost function of bacteria. Current position of robot, next position required and position of obstacle as detected by sensor were given as input to the algorithm and output produced was the most feasible path. So, results were produced after using this high level strategy. The algorithm works well in local environment where simple sensor was used. The results produced were compared with those produced by another well known algorithm PSO (Hossain & Ferdous, 2014). BFO algorithm was found to be better in terms of optimal path.

2.7.3 Parameter Estimation of Solar PV Model

Solar energy is available freely. Also, it is non-polluting. So, it has attracted the interest of many researchers. So, this attraction had given the birth to need for the photovoltaic module. But modeling photovoltaic panels is quite difficult because of the limited data as provided by the manufacturers. So, precise estimation of various modeling parameters was required to be established and that too in different environments for modeling photovoltaic panels accurately. Optimization techniques are useful to find solution of over determined systems (which has more variables then equations) or of non-linear system. Various algorithms like Artificial Immune System, Genetic Algorithm, and BFO was used (Krishnakumar, Venugopalan, & Rajasekar, 2013). They all were compared according to the performance based on various criteria. Some of criteria were accuracy, convergence speed, consistency etc. The results computed by each of these were compared with the actual values. All results were validated against photovoltaic modules namely multi crystalline and thin film. Best optimal value was again given by BFOA.

2.7.4 Application in Load Shedding

Optimization can also be applied to power system in field of load shedding. The basic goal was to remove some of the loads at fixed location in bus system. It was done to improve the loss of power and costs of shedded loads. The objective functions of total power losses, voltage stability index values and also total cost of shedded loads were used in determining the optimal load shedding in that particular system (Afif Wan, Rahman, & Zakaria, 2013). The technique was already implemented in IEEE-30 bus system. It was observed that algorithm gives better result when compared to the base case values of total power losses and voltage stability index values of that particular bus system.

2.7.5 Application in image registration

BFOA was applied on image registration as well as on multi-core processors. Image registration is one of the optimization problems. The goal was to compute the optimal parameters of one of the transform so as to align the source image to the model given in such a manner that similarities are maximized. Image registration is one of the important steps in the fusion of images. The reason being quality of fusion of image is affected by quality of result of image registration. Bacterial Foraging Optimization Algorithm can be used as image registration technique. But Image Registration becomes time consuming due to similarity measure and optimization algorithm used. So, this sequential algorithm can be converted to parallel on multi-core systems (Bejinariu, 2013). The parallel approach was based on shared memory model that can be implemented with ease in multi-core processors. Cost function which is a parameter in the algorithm implementation can be used in parallel on different cores.

2.7.6 Hybrid Least Square-Fuzzy Bacterial Foraging Strategy for Harmonic Estimation (Mishra, 2005)

BFOA has been used in power system to estimate the harmonic component in voltage or current waveforms. Depending on the operating conditions to make the convergence faster Takagi-Sugeno fuzzy scheme was used. Phase is non-linear while amplitude is linear in harmonic estimation. The overall scheme was hybrid in the sense linear least square estimates the amplitude and Newton-like gradient descent was applied to phase estimation. The percentage error and the time of processing were found to be improved as compared with the genetic algorithm and discrete Fourier transform. Performance was acceptable even with decaying dc component or change in phase angle or amplitude of harmonic estimation. Actually the non-linear part i.e. the phase of each harmonic was estimated by Fuzzy Bacterial Foraging (FBF) algorithm. Whereas, the linear part was estimated via normal least square estimator. For both GA and FBF scheme uses performance criteria as the cost function. Limitation of BBF was overcome by using Takagi-Sugeno fuzzy scheme. The algorithm showed better results than DFT in the noise. This was because the estimation problem becomes multimodal if noise is there so obviously FBF shows better results. Also since transducer noise is almost unavoidable in sampled signal so FBF shows the better performance than DFT algorithm. Also the time taken for convergence was almost half when compared to the genetic algorithm. So, overall it was better than both GA and DFT.

2.8 Modifications of Bacterial Foraging Optimization Algorithm

2.8.1 Hybridization with PSO (Particle Swarm Optimization)

Long et.al. has hybridized BFO with other algorithms so as to improve the accuracy, efficiency, and weak ability of the algorithm to come out of the local minima in the process of optimization. New proposed algorithm was formed by hybridization of BFO with well known algorithm PSO. Chemotaxis step of bacterial foraging was modified by merging it with PSO. Elimination Dispersal step of the algorithm was also modified. Resulting algorithm was proved better in terms of the accuracy, convergence speed. In PSO particles updates their position by using their local optimal as well as global optimal found upto now. This principle of PSO was merged in the chemotaxis of BFO. So, bacterium could compare its optimal point with the global optimal point i.e. obtained upto now. It swam in a particular direction if it keeps on getting better results than the optimal point. This accelerated the speed of algorithm to find the optimal point. PSO also replaces the random variable in the actual design. So, bacteria have improved by learning from itself as well as whole population. So, bacterium which was at good position will exploit the surrounding region while bacterium in bad region came to a better one with good speed. In elimination dispersal step, some or all of the bacteria are dispersed randomly. So, any of the good bacteria may get migrated to the new location. So, step was improved by eliminating the bacteria based on the life cycle energy. It improved the global searching time of the algorithm. The experimental data showed that: the improved hybrid particle swarm - bacterial foraging optimization algorithm is significantly better than individual particle swarm optimization algorithm and bacterial foraging optimization algorithm whether in searching speed or accuracy(Long, Jun, & Ping, 2010)

2.8.2 Self – Adapting BFOA

Chen et.al (Chen, Zhu, & Hu, 2008).has introduced the Self Adapting BFO. In standard BFOA all the bacteria has constant run-length. Self Adapting algorithm introduced the term exploration and exploitation. In the exploration step bacteria took large steps to move to the position which has higher nutrient value. In the exploitation step bacteria took small steps to exploit the particular region. Exploitation was done when bacteria was in the region with higher nutrient value. Bacterium changed its search behavior according to the environment i.e. bacteria adapted itself to the changing environment. It used two criteria. First one said whenever bacterium moved to the new promising domain its run length is decreased so as to exploit that reason properly. Second one said that bacterium enters the exploration so as to find some promising region. Four widely used benchmark functions have been used to test the SA-BFO algorithm in comparison with the original BFO, the standard PSO and the real-coded GA. The simulation results were encouraging: the SABFO was definitely better than the original BFO for all the test functions and appear to be comparable with the standard PSO and GA (Chen, Zhu, & Hu, 2008).

2.8.3 Parallel BFO

Pattnaik et.al. (Pattnaik, Bakwad, Devi, & Panig, 2011) proposed parallel BFO. In the original BFO basic steps in the chemotaxis were swimming and tumbling. Both of the steps resulted in updation of position and energy of bacteria. So, in the chemotaxis step each of the bacteria calculated its fitness. In parallel BFO fitness of each bacterium was computed in parallel manner. Master slave technology was used and number of slaves was equal to number of bacteria. Each of the slaves must report the computed fitness to the master. So that updated values could be used by other bacteria in the next chemotactic step. So, proper synchronization need to be ensured between master and slave. But there were some issues related to parallelization. All the slave nodes were required to work at same speed so that master may not wait for next operation. Synchronization was ensured properly so that overall fitness was not affected. The second change introduced was mutation operation after chemotaxis. This was done to accelerate the overall performance of PBFO. Positions were mutated by free PSO parameter. It did not require any other parameter or equation. The whole concept was introduced so as to decrease the computational time required to solve the high dimension function which are multimodal. (Pattnaik, Bakwad, Devi, & Panig, 2011) . Introduction of mutation improves the quality of global best.

2.8.4 Improved BFO

Chen et.al. (Chen & Lin, 2009) introduced the IBFO. The first change was made to the constant step size that was used in the algorithm. Bacteria used constant step size throughout the lifecycle in standard BFO. But it was more reasonable if larger step size is used in the beginning and smaller when bacterium is nearer to the global media as shown in eq. (2.1). So, step size was modified to

$$c(i) = c_{\max}(i) - \frac{c_{\max}(i) - c_{\min}(i)}{N_c} * j \qquad (2\text{-}1)$$

Where i is bacterium under consideration

$c_{\max}$ is maximum step size

$c_{\min}$ is minimum step size

N_c is total number of chemotactic steps

j is current chemotactic step.

J_{cc} was used in standard BFOA so as to produce the swarming effect. It used some parameters for attraction and repulsion. Attraction parameters were used so that good bacteria can attract other bacteria in the nutrient region and repulsion parameter was used so as to maintain certain minimal distance between two bacteria. But these attraction and repulsion parameters together resulted in oscillations in the bacterial movement. This J_{cc} was replaced by J_{gbest} which was the global optimal value obtained upto now. J_{gbest} has done two things. One produced the required swarming effect and second it replaced the J_{last}. J_{last} was maintaining local best information.

The third modification that was proposed was number of nutrients obtained by bacterium in its lifetime will not matter. In IBFO, particular bacterium has not been considered as the best if its final position is not close to the global optimal point and fitness of bacteria cannot be judged by the energy accumulated during lifetime. There was no need of calculating summation of energy. Bacteria were sorted against the value of fitness acquired in the last step only and healthier bacteria reproduced and rest died. It also saved computation time.

The last improvement that was made was narrowing the search space with the progress of algorithm. It has been observed that larger the search space less is the accuracy and more is the computational time. Search space is restricted according to the following equation

$$\theta_{\max}(j) = \theta_{gbest} + R/2^j \quad (2.2)$$

$$\theta_{\min}(j) = \theta_{gbest} - R/2^j \quad (2.3)$$

Where $\left[\theta_{\min}(j), \theta_{\max}(j)\right]$ is the current searching scope.

j is the current chemotaxis step.

R is the sphere of activity of swarm.

θ_{gbest} is updated while chemotaxis.

IBFO gave better performance than the classical BFO when tested over benchmark problems like Sphere, Rosenbrock, Rastrigin, Griewank. (Chen & Lin, 2009)

Chapter Three: **Biologically inspired algorithms: BFOA**

3.1 Introduction

Computing techniques are involved in various problems like pattern recognition, image recognition etc. In past, researchers used conventional computing techniques like hard computing technique to solve various problems. The problem with hard computing was that it requires exact computational model. Also data required to solve was needed to be accurate as well as precise. However in real world system it is not necessarily ideal. One more problem with hard computing technique was the time. Hard computing techniques required much time to develop. But hard computing techniques had been used widely by researchers and engineers.

In contrast soft computing techniques can be applied in many areas where hard computing techniques fail. Soft computing techniques don't require the data to be exact and accurate. Soft computing techniques can be used to solve real world problems. So we can apply soft computing techniques or methodologies in case of uncertainty, imprecision and partial truth. These advantages of Soft Computing over hard computing make it useful for wide range of application example machine performance prediction and optimization (Chandrasekaran, Muralidhar, Krishna, & Dixit, 2009) , in decision making problems (Roy & Maji, 2002).

Professor Zadeh's(Zadeh, 1965) original definition of soft computing is quoted below:

"*Soft computing differs from conventional (hard) computing in that, unlike hard computing, it is tolerant of imprecision, uncertainty, partial truth, and approximation. In effect, the role model for soft computing is the human mind. The guiding principle of soft computing is: Exploit the tolerance for imprecision, uncertainty, partial truth, and approximation to achieve tractability, robustness and low solution cost. At this juncture, the principal constituents of soft computing (SC) are fuzzy logic (FL), neural computing (NC), genetic computing (GC) and probabilistic reasoning (PR), with the latter subsuming belief networks, chaos theory and parts of learning theory. What is important to note is that soft computing is not a melange. Rather, it is a partnership in which of the partners contributes a distinct methodology for addressing problems in its domain. In this prospective, the principal constituent methodologies in SC are complementary rather than competitive.*"

The main constituents of soft computing are Neural Network, Probabilistic Reasoning, Fuzzy Logic and Genetic Computing. Soft computing gives better results generally when we use mixture of above constituent rather than using single of above constituent. Soft computing can be used in place of hard computing in some of the techniques and in some other techniques it can be used along with hard computing. We need both Soft Computing and Hard Computing whenever we want a solution that is cost effective and accurate.

3.2 Biologically Inspired Algorithms

We need to find the global optimum in case of optimization problems. But there are several problems associated with this. For example our search space is too large, there are many local optima, and it may take large computation time. Many tools are developed to solve such problems. Both deterministic and heuristic approach can be used in this regard. Deterministic algorithm search for the optimum point using some well defined procedure while heuristic approaches proceed based on the experience gained. If we compare both the approaches then deterministic gives high possibility to find the solution but obviously in more computation time than heuristic. Heuristic approaches are non deterministic and hence they search for global optima randomly but within some reasonable time. But if problem required to be solved is highly complex and non-linear then computation process increases significantly in this case also. Biologically-inspired algorithms come under soft computing methodologies. They are developed by mimicking natural algorithms or more appropriately biological algorithms as that of natural selection, foraging etc. The aim was to develop alternating technique to solve highly complex problems or to solve over-determined systems (one with more variables then equations). These systems cannot be solved using usual methods like gradient descent method. All the process that occurs in nature are very efficient and optimal. So, it's a good idea to mimic these processes as algorithms and use in our problems. Below in **Error! Reference source not found.** the hierarchy of biologically inspired algorithms is shown.

Biologically inspired algorithms mimic the behaviour of animals that they exhibit in some sort of group activity like foraging. Particle Swarm Optimization, Ant Colony Optimization, Artificial Bee Colony Optimization are some of the algorithms developed on this ground. BFOA(Bacterial Foraging Optimization Algorithm) is an another algorithm which was given by Passino (Passino K. M., 2002). It has been used widely in many of the engineering problem related to optimization example harmonic estimation (Mishra, 2005), Parameter estimation of Wiener model (Huang & Lin, 2010).

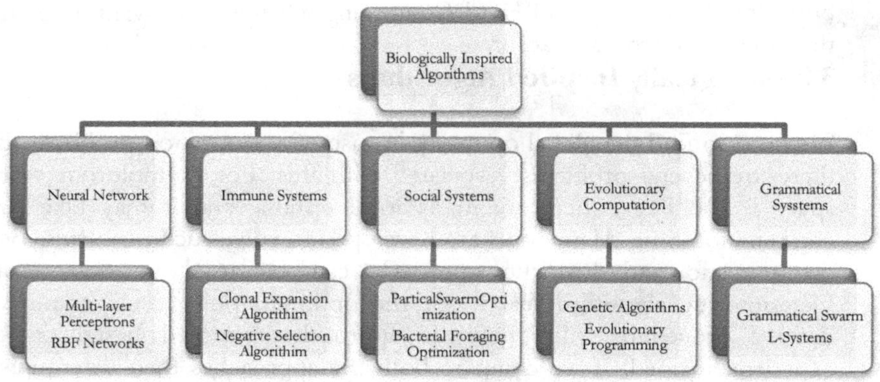

Figure 3.1 Block diagram showing hierarchy of biologically inspired algorithm

Bacterial Foraging Optimization Algorithm was developed to mimic the foraging strategy of Escherichia Coli Bacteria. E. Coli is a rod shaped bacteria that is found in lower intestine of warm blooded organisms. E.Coli always tries to move to place which has highest amount of nutrition, avoiding the harmful environment. If we map this to optimization problem then bacteria will have to move to position of highest energy and this position will be required optimum position. Bacteria can initially be placed at any of the random positions in the search space. Bacteria will move in the search space in order to find the optimum value. Process by which a bacterium moves from one position to another position in order to a find position with highest nutrient value is known as chemotaxis. Bacteria exhibit two operations in chemotaxis namely swimming and tumbling. Bacterium uses flagella for swimming and tumbling. In each chemotactic step bacterium gets some energy. Each bacterium undergoes certain fixed number of chemotact steps. After this health which is sum of energy obtained at each chemotactic step of each bacterium is calculated and bacteria are sorted according to this health. Bacterium with least energy and best health is considered to be the bacteria with highest nutrient value. So half of the healthy bacteria reproduce on finding suitable conditions into two and remaining half are eliminated. So, theory of natural selection is applicable here. Finally, sometimes due to occurrence of some rare event like sudden rise in temperature etc. some of the bacteria may be migrated to some media.

3.2.1 Escherichia Coli Bacteria

BFOA is an optimization algorithm used for optimization was developed based on the foraging behaviour of Escherichia Coli bacteria found in lower intestine of warm blooded organisms. Foraging is the process by which animals locate and ingest their food. The structure of E. Coli bacteria is shown in Figure 3.2 below. In suitable environment whenever E. Coli gets longer it splits into two parts. For example on getting sufficient food and temperature of around 37 degree centigrade it can develop everything it needs to replicate within 20 minutes. Hence in short time population can be doubled easily. It also has some sort of system that guides its search for food and help avoiding noxious environment. It will swim from noxious environment to healthy environment.

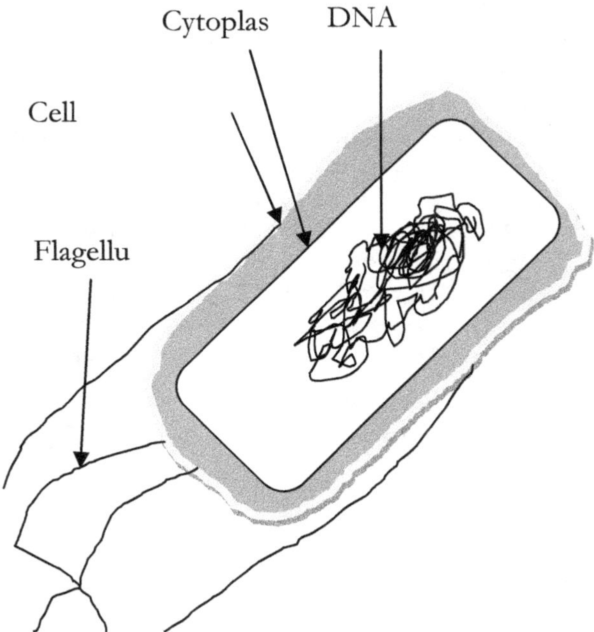

Figure 3.2 Coli Bacteria Structure

3.2.1.1 Basic Concept of Movement of Bacteria

E. Coli bacteria always tries to move to the position where there is highest value of nutrition avoiding poisonous environment side by side. This motion of E. Coli in order to find the most optimum position is known as chemotaxis. Tumble and Swimming are the two basic operations exhibited by bacteria in chemotaxis. Straight movement is known as swimming and if bacterium changes its direction then it is known as tumbling. Less energy is here associated with higher nutrition value. So, lesser the energy more is the nutrition value and higher the energy less is the nutrition value. Therefore, ultimate goal is to reach at the position with highest nutrient value or lowest energy. Now, bacteria move in straight direction if its energy continues to decrease i.e. its health continues to improve. It tumbles if there is no improvement in energy, and in case of poisonous environment it tumbles more. In short, if bacteria found improvement in energy with respect to previous position it swims otherwise, it tumbles.

Below Figure 3.3 depicts the swim and Figure 3.4 depicts tumble in bacteria. Considering Figure 3.3 bacterium is initially at position P_1 with energy E_1 at this position energy is. Now the bacterium moves to position P_2. Energy changes with change in position here again energy of bacterium is calculated. Suppose new energy is E_2. Now, this new energy is compared with old energy. If new energy is less than previous energy bacterium continues to move in that direction. In this way bacterium swims in particular direction i.e. it swims from position P_1 to P_2 and from P_2 to P_3. In Figure 3.4 bacterium moves forward from position P_1 to P_2. Energy initially at P_1 is $E_1$and at P_2 is E_2. Both E_1 and E_2 are compared. In this case E_2 is greater than E_1. So, bacterium tumbles in the random direction and moves to P_3. Energy of P_3 is compared to best energy reached by this bacterium till now i.e. E_3 is compared to the E_1. Again energy E_3 is greater than E_1. So, bacterium will tumble again in some random direction and reach at position P_4. Again since position of bacterium is updated energy is calculated. Suppose energy at P_4 is E_4. E_4 is compared to E_1.Value of E_4 is lower than that of E_1 so bacteria will now move in this direction. It swims to position P_5 and whole chemotaxis cycle continues like this.

3.2.2 Constituent steps in the life cycle of bacteria

Each bacterium undergoes four main steps during its life cycle namely:

- Chemotaxis
- Swarming
- Reproduction
- Elimination Dispersal

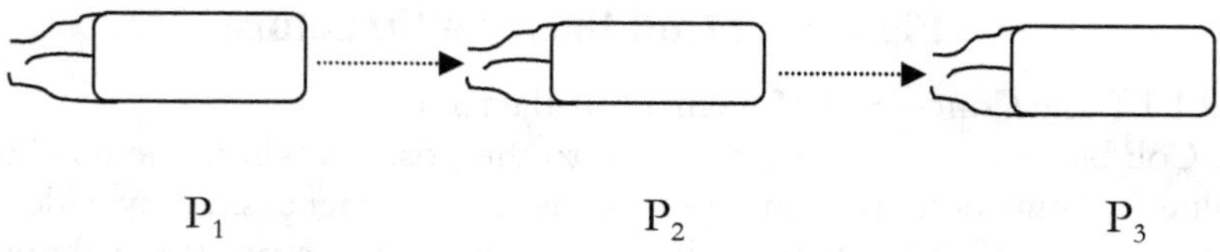

Figure 3.3 Chemotaxis- Swimming

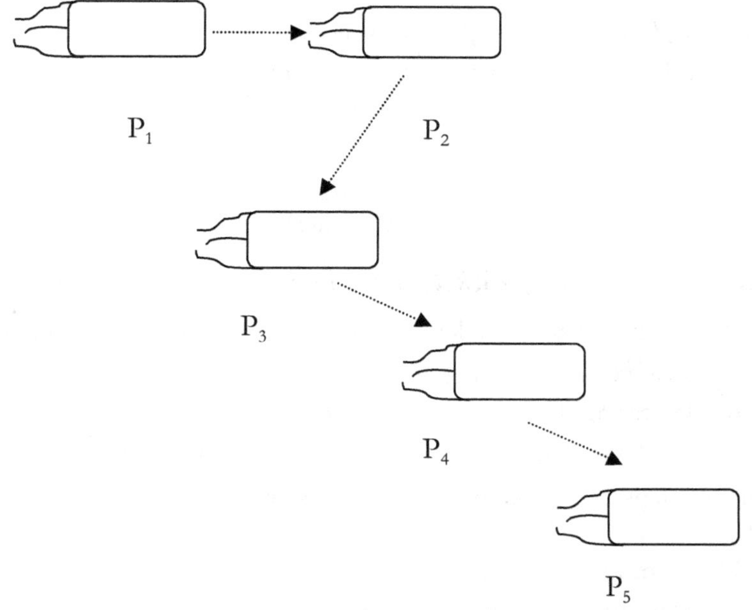

Figure 3.4 Chemotaxis- Tumbling

3.2.2.1 Chemotaxis

Chemotaxis stands for movement by a cell or organism in reaction to a chemical stimulus. This step simulates the movement of bacteria in the search space. Chemotaxis basically constitutes two main steps swimming and tumbling. Depending on the medium in which it is searching for food bacteria can:

- Swim followed by tumble
- Tumble followed by swim
- Tumble followed by tumble
- Swim continuously

The position of bacteria can be represented by $\theta^{i}(j,k,l)$ where i,j,k,l means i^{th} bacterium at j^{th} chemotactic, k^{th} reproductive and l^{th} elimination-dispersal step. Amount of movement in particular direction is quantified by a parameter know as step size $C(i)$ where i is the bacteria under consideration. If value of $C(i)$ is kept large then algorithm may jump over the optimum point and if value of $C(i)$ is small then algorithm may take large time to converge. Energy of bacteria is represented by $J(j,k,l)$ where j,k,l means at j^{th} chemotactic, k^{th} reproductive and l^{th} elimination-dispersal step. Whenever bacterium needs to tumble a random unit vector Δ is generated such that Δ [-1,1].Finally, Motion of bacteria can be represented mathematically as:

$$\theta^i(j+1,k,l) = \theta^i(j,k,l) + c(i)\frac{\Delta(i)}{\sqrt{\Delta^{\mathrm{T}}(i)\Delta(i)}} \tag{3-1}$$

If value of energy $J(j+1,k,l)$ at $\theta^i(j+1,k,l)$ is lower than $J(j,k,l)$ at $\theta^i(j,k,l)$ then bacteria takes one step forward in the same direction with step size $c(i)$ and will continue to swim in that direction if energy keeps on decreasing. But maximum number of times bacteria can swim in particular direction is given by N_s where N_s is the maximum number of swimming steps. After completion of N_s steps bacterium will have to tumble.

3.2.2.2 Swarming

While moving bacteria can release chemical substances so that other bacteria can be attracted and they could swarm together. Foraging is group activity and group behavior is governed by these chemicals. They could release a sort of repellent also. So that, no two bacteria can be on the same position at same instant of time. Repellent ensures that there is some particular amount of distance between two bacteria. So, swarming justifies group behavior by cell-to-cell signaling or by attractant and repellents. This is how bacteria swarm together. Mathematically swarming can be represented as:

$$J_{cc}(\theta, P(j,k,l)) = \sum_{i=1}^{S} J_{cc}(\theta, \theta^i(j,k,l))$$

$$= \sum_{i=1}^{S}\left[-d_{attractant}\exp\left(-w_{attractant}\sum_{m=1}^{p}(\theta_m - \theta_m^i)^2\right)\right] + \sum_{i=1}^{S}\left[-h_{repellent}\exp\left(-w_{repellent}\sum_{m=1}^{p}(\theta_m - \theta_m^i)^2\right)\right] \tag{3-2}$$

where,

$J_{cc}(\theta, P(j,k,l))$ is the objective function (to be minimized).

S represents the total number of bacteria.

p is number of dimension of the space in which bacteria will move or it is number of parameters required to be optimized.

$\theta = \left[\theta_1, \theta_2 .....\theta_p \right]^{T}$ is a particular point in the search domain with p dimension.

$d_{attractant}$ it gives the depth to which attractant is released or it quantifies the attractant released.

$w_{attractant}$ it gives the width of attractant i.e. it quantifies the magnitude to which it effects.

$h_{repellent}$ it gives the depth to which repellent is released or it quantifies the repellent released.

$w_{repellent}$ it gives the width of repellent i.e. it quantifies the magnitude to which it effects.

If value of $d_{attractant}$ and $w_{attractant}$ is too high means there is large magnitude and height of attraction. So, bacteria will swarm in group. But they may miss some of the nutrients. Very less value of these will not introduce group behaviour. Hence they will not swarm together and search for food independently. So, optimum value of these parameters is required to be set so that optimum amount of swarming is introduced. Value of these parameters lies in between [1, 9] and should be chosen appropriately.

3.2.2.3 Reproduction

Bacteria reproduce very fast in the nutrient media so population size will increase. Similarly, in poor nutrient media bacteria will die rapidly resulting in decrease in population. After N_c chemotactic steps health of each bacteria is calculated by adding the energies accumulated at each chemotactic step. Lower the value of J_{health} more fit is the bacteria or medium is nutrient. Higher J_{health} value signifies bacteria are unfit or nutrient is poor. So bacteria in nutrient medium tend to reproduce and bacteria with poor nutrients tend to die. To keep the algorithm simple it is assumed that half of the bacteria with lower J_{health} value will reproduce and half of the bacteria with higher J_{health} value will die. In this way total population size remains constant. So, finally bacteria with low J_{health} value die and other asexually split into two.

$$J^i_{health} = \sum_{j=1}^{N_c} J(i,j,k,l)$$
$$S_r = \frac{S}{2} \tag{3-3}$$

It is assumed that we have even number of bacteria. So, finally bacteria S_r with lower J_{health} will reproduce and other S_r will die and new S_r bacteria will be placed at same position as their parents.

3.2.2.4 Elimination dispersal

Occasionally when there are sudden changes in the local environment like sudden change in temperature some of the bacteria which are present in the search space may be migrated to some other location. Sometimes all the bacteria may be migrated to some other location. Algorithmically a probability P_{ed} is considered. It's a random probability and its value lies between 0 and 1. Apart from this, a random probability is generated corresponding to each bacterium. This probability is compared to P_{ed} . If its value is lower than P_{ed} then this bacterium will migrate to some new location. However, to keep the algorithm simple some other bacterium is migrated to search space at some random position. This phase of bacteria's life cycle helps the algorithm to come out of local minima and to exploit the positions not exploited yet.

3.3 Bacterial Foraging Optimization Algorithm

Originally the BFOA was proposed by Passino in the year 2002 (Passino K. , 2002) after that many modifications are made in the standard algorithm. **Table 3.1**shows that parameters used in this algorithm, it has parameter names along with their corresponding description.

Let position of each bacterium in the population of size S is represented by $P(j,k,l)=\{\theta^i(j,k,l), i=1,2....S\}$ where j means at j^{th} chemotactic step, k means at k^{th} reproduction step, and l means at l^{th} elimination-dispersal step. Here, let $J(i,j,k,l)$ denote the energy of ith bacterium position $\theta^i(j,k,l) \in \Re^{\mathrm{P}}$. J can be termed both as energy of bacteria at particular position or as cost which is to be minimized. In nature value of S i.e. number of bacteria in population can be very large but number of dimensions is restricted to be 4. But in case of simulation number of bacteria in population is kept fixed and is small. However value of p i.e. dimensions of search space can be greater than 3 depending on the number of parameters required to be optimized in the problem.

Table 3.1 Parameters used in BFOA (Das, Biswas, Dasgupta, & Abraham, 2009)

S.NO.	PARAMETER NAME	DESCRIPTION
1	j	the variable used as loop counter for chemotactic step
2	k	the variable used as loop counter for reproduction step
3	l	the variable used as loop counter for elimination dispersal step
4	p	Dimension of the search space
5	S	Total number of bacteria in the population
6	N_c	The number of chemotactic steps
7	N_s	The swimming length
8	N_{re}	The number of reproduction steps
9	N_{ed}	The number of elimination-dispersal events
10	P_{ed}	Elimination-dispersal probability
11	$c(i)$	The size of the step taken in the random direction specified by the tumble

The algorithm is as follows (Das, Biswas, Dasgupta, & Abraham, 2009)

[Step 1] Initialize parameters $p, S, N_c, N_{re}, N_{ed}, N_s, c(i), P_{ed}$ where $i = 1, 2, ...S$

[Step 2] Elimination-dispersal loop: $l = l + 1$

[Step 3] Reproduction loop: $k = k + 1$

[Step 4] Chemotaxis loop: $j = j + 1$

[a] For $i = 1, 2, ...S$ take a chemotactic step for bacterium *i* as follows.

[b] Compute fitness function, $J(i, j, k, l)$

Let, $J(i, j, k, l) = J(i, j, k, l) + Jcc(\theta^i(j, k, l), P(j, k, l))$ (i.e. add on the cell-to cellattractant–repellent profile to simulate the swarming behaviour)where, J_{cc} is defined in(3.2).

[c] Let $J_{last} = J(i, j, k, l)$ to save this value since we may find a better cost via a run.

[d] Tumble: generate a random vector $\Delta(i) \in \Re^p$ with each element $\Delta_m(i)$, $m = 1, 2, ...p$ a random number on $[-1, 1]$.

[e] Move: Let

$$\theta^i(j+1,k,l)=\theta^i(j,k,l)+c(i)\frac{\Delta(i)}{\sqrt{\Delta^T(i)\Delta(i)}}$$

This results in a step of size $c(i)$ in the direction of the tumble for bacterium i.

[f] Compute $J(i,j+1,k,l)$ and let,

$$J(i,j+1,k,l)=J(i,j,k,l)+J_{cc}(\theta^i(j+1,k,l),P(j+1,k,l)) \quad (3.6)$$

[g] Swim

i) Let $m=0$ (counter for swim length).

ii) While $m<N_s$ (if have not climbed down too long).

• Let $m=m+1$.

• If $J(i,j+1,k,l)<J_{last}$ (if doing better), let $J_{last}=J(i,j+1,k,l)$ and let

$$\theta^i(j+1,k,l)=\theta^i(j,k,l)+c(i)\frac{\Delta(i)}{\sqrt{\Delta^T(i)\Delta(i)}}$$ use this $\theta^i(j+1,k,l)$ to compute the new $J(i,j+1,k,l)$ as we did in [f]

• Else, let $m=N_s$ This is the end of the while statement.

[h] Go to next bacterium (i+1) if $i<S$ (i.e., go to [b] to process the next bacterium).

[Step 5] If $j<N_c$, go to step 4. In this case continue chemotaxis since the life of the bacteria is not over.

[Step 6] Reproduction:

[a] For the given k and l, and for each $i=1,2,...S$, let

$$J^i_{health}=\sum_{j=1}^{N_c+1}J(i,j,k,l)$$

be the health of the bacterium i (a measure of how many nutrients it got over its lifetime and how successful it was at avoiding noxious substances). Sort bacteria and chemotactic parameters $c(i)$ in order of ascending cost J_{health} (higher cost means lower health).

[b] The S_r bacteria with the highest J_{health} values die and the remaining S_r bacteria with the best values split (this process is performed by the copies that are made are placed at the same location as their parent).

[Step 7] If $k < N_{re}$ go to step 3. In this case, we have not reached the number of specified reproduction steps, so we start the next generation of the chemotactic loop.

[Step 8] Elimination-dispersal: For $i = 1, 2, ...S$ with probability P_{ed}, eliminate and disperse each bacterium (this keeps the number of bacteria in the population constant). To do this, if a bacterium is eliminated, simply disperse another one to a random location on the optimization domain. If $l < N_{ed}$, then go to step 2; otherwise end.

3.3.1 Guidelines for choosing the parameter

There are many parameters used in the algorithm and each of the parameter may influence the algorithm in different ways. Different parameters are described below:

3.3.1.1 Number of Bacteria S

Suppose a large value of S is taken i.e. large number of bacteria. In this case computational complexity of the algorithm will increase. But chances of finding an accurate solution will also increase. It may happen in starting itself that some of the bacteria are near to the optimal value.

3.3.1.2 Step Size $c(i)$

Biologically motivated value may be chosen but it may not be best according to the engineering problem. If value of $c(i)$ is kept large then algorithm may jump over the optimum point and if value of $c(i)$ is small then algorithm may take large time to converge increasing the computational complexity.

3.3.1.3 J_{cc} parameters

J_{cc} parameters influence the swarm and independent foraging behaviour of bacteria. If value of $d_{attractant}$, $h_{repellent}$, $w_{repellent}$ and $w_{attractant}$ is too high means there is large magnitude and height of attraction. So, bacteria will swarm in group. But they may miss some of the nutrients. Very less value of these will not introduce group behaviour. Hence they will not swarm together and search for food independently. Therefore, optimum value of these parameters is required to be set so that optimum amount of swarming is introduced. Value of these parameters lie in between [1, 9] and should be chosen appropriately. Thus, they influence characteristics of swarming.

3.3.1.4 Number of Chemotactic Steps N_c

Increasing the value of N_c may result in better optimization results but it will increase the computational complexity as well. However, low value of

N_c may result in dependence of optimization more on luck and reproduction.

3.3.1.5 Number of Reproduction Steps N_{re}

Reproduction steps helps to ignore bad regions by killing bacteria will poor nutrients. However, large value may increase the computational complexity.

3.3.1.6 Number of Elimination Dispersal Steps N_{ed}

Low value of N_{ed} indicates that algorithm rely less on random elimination dispersal step to find the solution. However, high value increases computational complexity and also helps in exhaustive search. It can help algorithm to jump out of local minima and search for global optima. Therefore, optimum value of N_{ed} allows algorithm to look in more regions.

3.3.1.7 Number of swimming steps N_s

The value for this parameter is chosen as optimal because increasing its value will increase the complexity of the algorithm while decreasing its value will create a problem in converging of the algorithm.

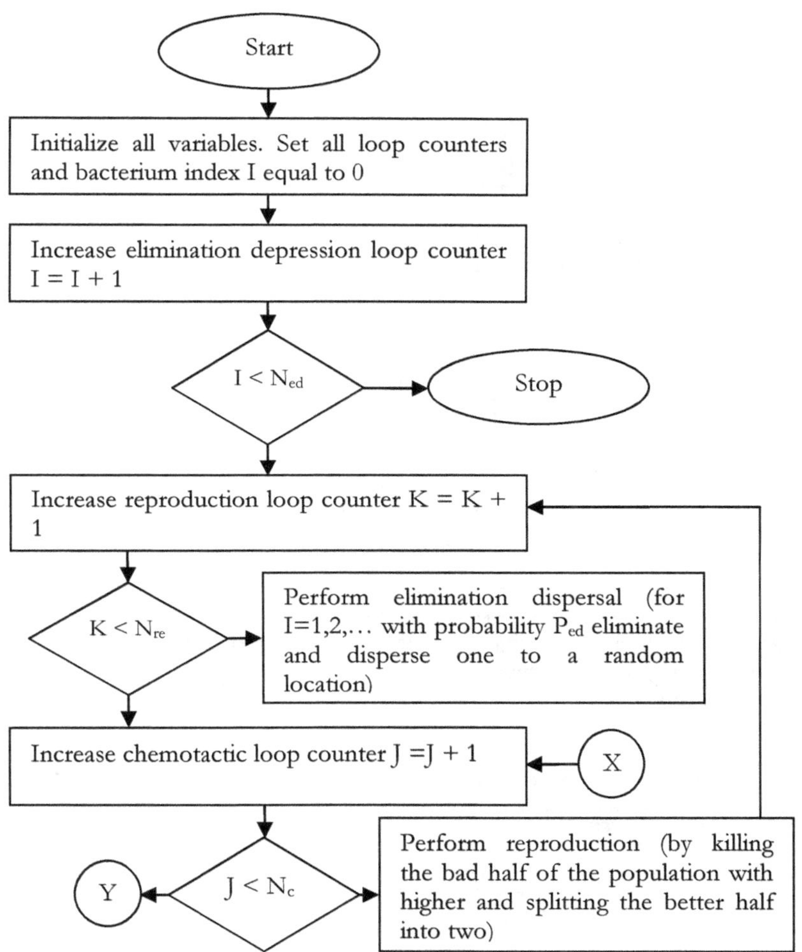
Start
Initialize all variables. Set all loop counters and bacterium index I equal to 0
Increase elimination depression loop counter I = I + 1
I < Ned
Stop
Increase reproduction loop counter K = K + 1
K < Nre
Perform elimination dispersal (for I=1,2,... with probability Ped eliminate and disperse one to a random location)
Increase chemotactic loop counter J =J + 1
X
Y
J < Nc
Perform reproduction (by killing the bad half of the population with higher and splitting the better half into two)

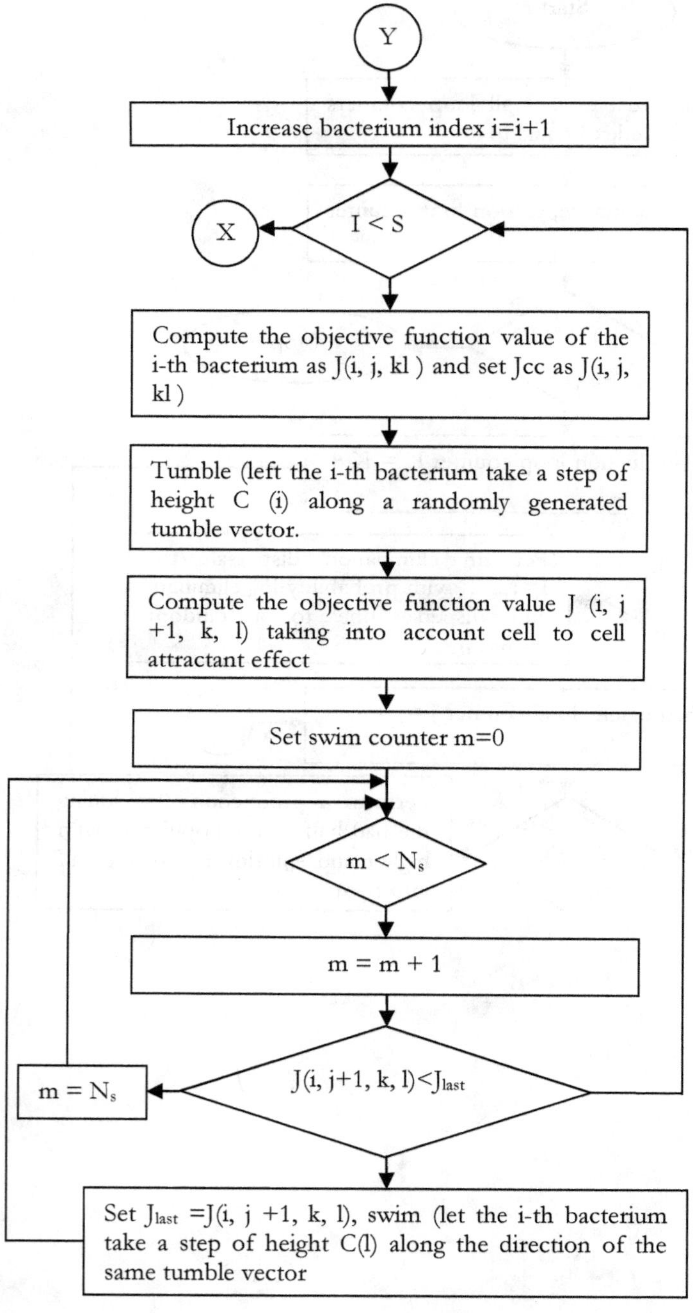
Y
Increase bacterium index i=i+1
X
I < S
Compute the objective function value of the i-th bacterium as J(i, j, kl) and set Jcc as J(i, j, kl)
Tumble (left the i-th bacterium take a step of height C (i) along a randomly generated tumble vector.
Compute the objective function value J (i, j +1, k, l) taking into account cell to cell attractant effect
Set swim counter m=0
m < Ns
m = m + 1
m = Ns
J(i, j+1, k, l)<Jlast
Set Jlast =J(i, j +1, k, l), swim (let the i-th bacterium take a step of height C(l) along the direction of the same tumble vector

Chapter Four: **BAT Optimization**

The selection of a best element from some set of available alternatives with regard to some criteriain known as Optimization or mathematical programming. (The Nature of Mathematical Programming)

An optimization problem generally consists of maximizing or minimizing a real function by systematically choosing input values from a well defined domain or a set of constraints and consequently computing the value of the function.

Optimization problems are of various types:

- Discrete optimization:

In this the variables used in the optimization are restricted to assume only a finite or discrete set of values, such as the integers.

- Continuous Optimization:

In continuous optimization the variables used in the objective function can assume real values, e.g., values from intervals of the real line.

We can classify these algorithms into various types. Further we illustrate the classification in Figure 4.1

We are going to study Meta Heuristic Algorithms in detail as Bat Algorithm is one of the meta-heuristic and nature inspired Algorithm.

4.1 Meta-heuristic algorithms

Meta-heuristic algorithms are high level procedure which is designed to find or generate a low level procedure which may provide a sufficiently good solution to optimize a problem. We also need not to have complete information about the problem to get a solution. Thus we can conclude that "Meta-" means "beyond" or "higher level" and "heuristic" means "search" or "discover by trial or error".

Meta-heuristic algorithms usually consist of two major processes, i.e., solution exploration and solution exploitation. These two processes are iteratively performed to search for optimal or near-optimal solutions in reasonable computation time. The exploration process not only increases the diversity of solutions found, but also helps to overcome local optimal solutions to obtain better or optimal ones due to its randomization.(X.S., 2008)

To improve the quality of solutions obtained from the exploration process and to ensure that the solution converge to optimality, we use Exploitation. In some meta-heuristic algorithms, this exploitation process also helps to overcome local optimal solutions to search for better or optimal ones. The performance of meta-heuristic algorithms depends on the appropriate combination between these two processes (Exploration and Exploitation).

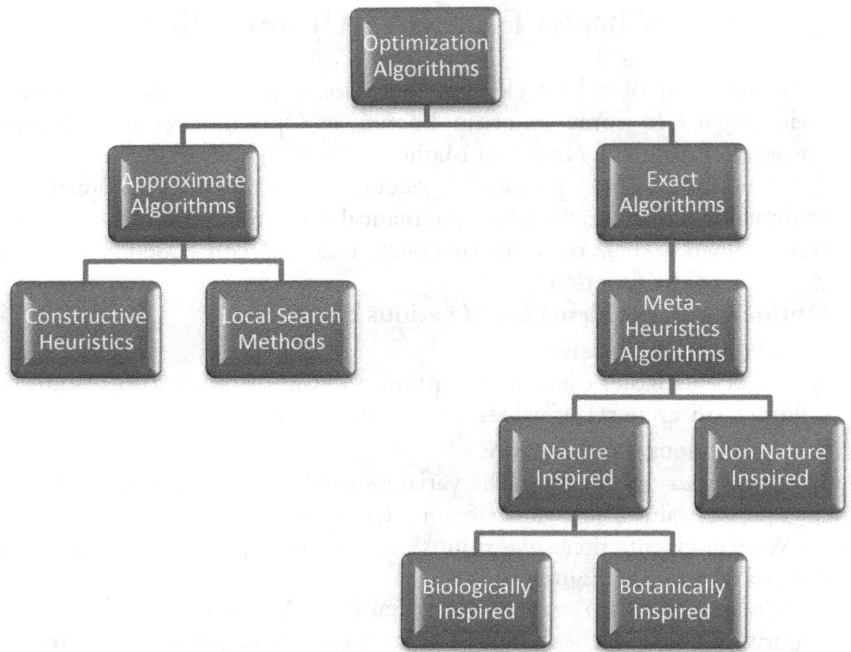

Figure 4.1: Classification of Optimization Algorithms

We have classified meta-heuristic algorithms into two major types, i.e., nature-inspired algorithms and non-nature inspired algorithms. Nature has been evolving for millions of years and hence learning from the nature's success, we can design meta-heuristic algorithms (X.S., 2008). Nature-inspired algorithms can be further divided into biologically inspired algorithms, botanically inspired algorithms. In Nature inspired algorithms we are going to focus mainly on biologically inspired algorithms.

4.2 Biologically inspired algorithms

These algorithms are inspired by creatures in nature and they are further classified into three major groups: evolutionary algorithms, stigmergic optimization algorithms, and swarm-based optimization algorithms as illustrated in Figure 4.2

Evolutionary Algorithms

Evolutionary algorithms are based on the principles of natural evolution. Natural evolution is a complex process which operates on chromosomes, instead of organisms (Michalewicz, 1992). The chromosomes contain genetic information, called a gene, which is passed from one generation to next generation through reproduction. In reproduction, the most important operators are recombination and mutation. Organisms with good chromosomes have a higher chance to exist and develop in nature.

According to Darwin's natural selection theory (Darwin, 1859), natural selection process selects best environment-adapted organisms.

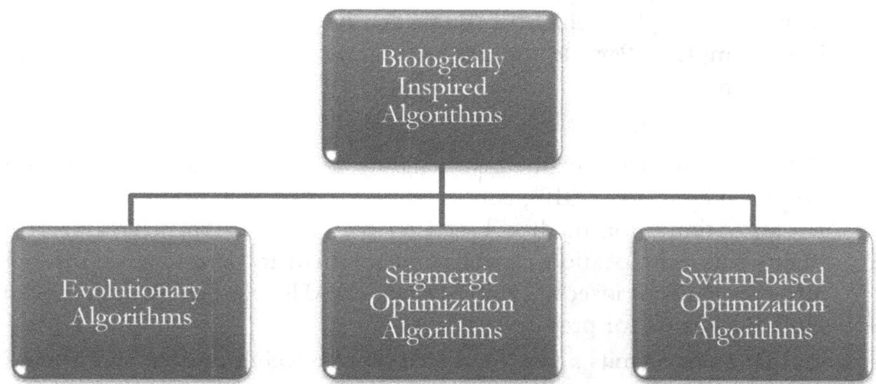

Figure 4.2: Biologically Inspired Algorithms

Evolutionary Algorithms

Evolutionary algorithms are based on the principles of natural evolution. Natural evolution is a complex process which operates on chromosomes, instead of organisms (Michalewicz, 1992). The chromosomes contain genetic information, called a gene, which is passed from one generation to next generation through reproduction. In reproduction, the most important operators are recombination and mutation. Organisms with good chromosomes have a higher chance to exist and develop in nature. According to Darwin's natural selection theory (Darwin, 1859), natural selection process selects best environment-adapted organisms.
For example: Genetic algorithm (GA)

- **Stigmergic Optimization Algorithms**

According to (Abraham A., 2006) Self-Organization insects often require interactions among themselves and such interactions can be direct or indirect. Direct interactions are the quite obvious interactions like food or liquid exchange, visual contact, chemical contact (the odour of nearby nest mates), etc. In Indirect interactions between two individuals interact indirectly when one of them modifies the environment and the other responds to the new environment at a later time. This type of interaction is called as "stigmergy".
For example: Termite algorithm, Ant colony optimization and Bee colony optimization.

- **Swarm-Based Optimization Algorithms**

Swarm-based optimization algorithms are inspired by the social behaviour of swarm-based animals or insects, such as a school of fish or a flock of

birds, especially those in which the property of historical information exchange among individuals is magnified. These algorithms use many autonomous agents (particles) that act together in simple ways to produce seemingly complex behaviour.(Banks A., 2007)
For example: Particle swarm optimization, Firefly algorithm and Bat algorithm.

4.2.1 Bat algorithm

Bat algorithm is a meta-heuristic, nature inspired, swarm based algorithm proposed by (Yang, 2010), and its categorization is illustrated in Figure 4.3. It's an optimization method based on the echolocation behaviour of bats. Micro bats echolocation capability helps them to detect preys, distinguish different kinds of insects, avoid obstacles, and locate their prey in the dark.
How Bat search for prey

- These bats emits a very loud sound pulse (echolocation) and listens the echo that bounces back from the surrounding objects as illustrated in Figure 4.4.
- Bats use short frequency-modulated signals to catch prey.
- Each Bat has a constant frequency of emitted pulse which is usually in the region of 25 kHz to 150 kHz.
- Each ultrasonic burst may last typically 5 to 20 ms, and micro bats emit about 10 to 20 such sound bursts every second.
- With time as bat moves toward prey, it changes its velocity and position to get more near about prey.

As the bat goes near prey, the rate of pulse emission increases which can be up to about 200 pulses per second and loudness decreases.

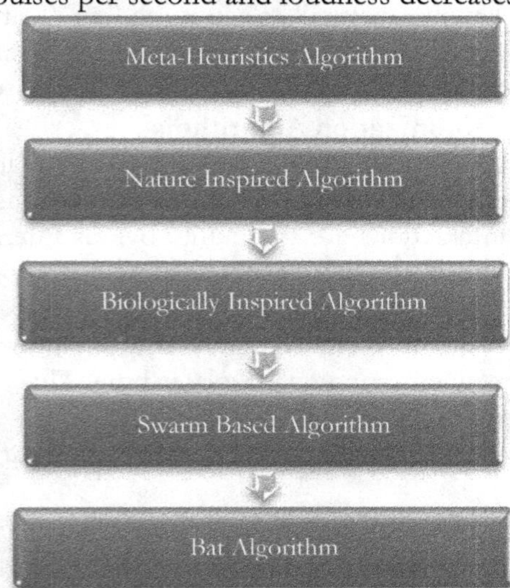

Figure 4.3:Categorization of Bat Algorithm

This property of bat can be used to propose various algorithms and finally proposed algorithm comes out with following idealized rules:

- All bats use echolocation to sense distance, and they also 'know' the difference between food/prey
- Bats fly randomly with velocity v_i at position x_i with a fixed frequency f_{min}, varying wavelength and loudness A_0 to search for prey. They can automatically adjust the wavelength (or frequency) of their emitted pulses and adjust the rate of pulse emission r [0, 1], depending on prey position.
- We also use the following approximations, for simplicity. In general the frequency f in a range [f_{min}, f_{max}] corresponds to a range of wavelengths [λ_{min}, λ_{max}]. For example a frequency range of [20 kHz, 500 kHz] corresponds to a range of wavelengths from 0.7mm to 17mm.
- Although the loudness can vary in many ways, we assume that the loudness varies from a large (positive) A_0 to a minimum constant value Amin. Pulse rate increases as the bat approaches prey.

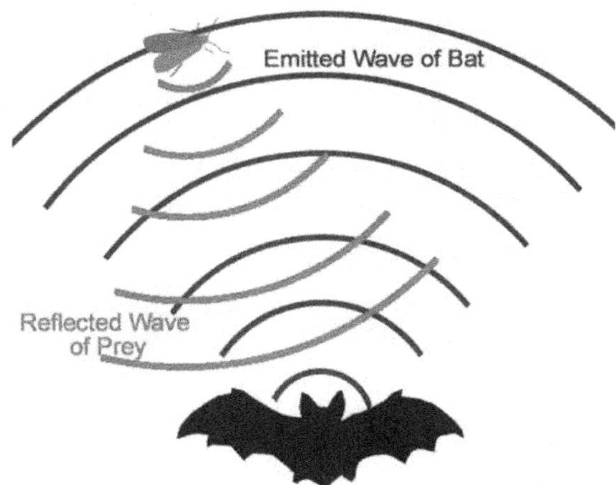

Figure 4.4 : Bat using echolocation to catch its prey

Pseudo code of the bat algorithm (BAT)

Objective function $f(x), x = (x_1 ... x_d)^T$ (4-1)

Initialize the bat population:
Initialize position, x_i (i = 1, 2... n bats) and velocity v_i
Define pulse rate (r_i), loudness (A_i) and frequency (f_i) for all bats
While (t <Max number of iterations)
  Generate new solutions by adjusting frequency,
  And updating velocities and locations/solutions
  If (rand >r_i)
    Select a solution among the best solutions

Generate a local solution around the selected best solution
End if
Generate a new solution by flying randomly
If (rand < A_i&&f (x_i) < f(x_*))
Accept the new solutions
Increase $r_i$and reduce A_i
End iRank the bats and find the current best x_*
End while
Post process results and visualization

Movement of Virtual Bats

For simulations, we use virtual bats naturally. Their positions x_i and velocities v_i in a d-dimensional search space has to be updated and for that we use following equations. The new Solutions x_i and velocities v_i at time step t is given by:

$$\mathbf{f_i = f_{min} + (f_{max} - f_{min})\beta}$$
$$\mathbf{v_i^t = v_i^{t-1} + (x_i^t - x_*)f_i}$$
$$\mathbf{x_i^t = x_i^{t-1} + v_i^t}$$

Where, β= [0, 1] is a random vector drawn from a uniform distribution. Here x_* is the Current global best location (solution) which is located after comparing all the solutions among all the n bats. We can use either f_i or λ_i to adjust the velocity change while fixing the other factor.

For the local search part, once a solution is selected among the current best solutions, a new solution for each bat is generated locally using random walk

$$\mathbf{X_{new} = X_{old} + \epsilon A^t}$$

Where ϵ is [−1, 1] is a random number, while $A^t$is the average loudness of all the bats at this time step.

Loudness and Pulse Emission

The loudness A_i and the rate r_i of pulse emission have to be updated accordingly as the iterations proceed. As the loudness usually decreases once a bat has found its prey, while the rate of pulse emission increases, the loudness can be chosen as any value of convenience. We can also use A_{max} = 1 and A_{min} = 0, assuming A_{min} = 0 means that a bat has just found the prey and temporarily stop emitting any sound.

$$\mathbf{A_i^{t+1} = \alpha A_i^t, \quad r_i^{t+1} = r_i^0[1 - \exp(-\gamma t)]},$$

Where αand ϒare constants with values: 0 <α<1 andϒ>0

Initially, each bat should have different values of loudness and pulse emission rate, and this can be achieved by randomization.

Flow of algorithm, is illustrated in Figure 4.5.

Variants of bat algorithm

In order to improve the performance, many methods and strategies have been attempted to increase the diversity of the solution and thus to enhance the performance, which produced a few good variants of bat algorithm..

- Fuzzy Logic Bat Algorithm (FLBA): (Khan, 2011) presented a variant by introducing fuzzy logic into the bat algorithm; they called their variant fuzzy bat algorithm.
- Multi objective bat algorithm (MOBA):(Yang X. S., 2011)extended BA to deal with multi objective optimization, which has demonstrated its effectiveness for solving a few design benchmarks in engineering.
- K-Means Bat Algorithm (KMBA):(Komarasamy, 2012)presented a combination of K-means and bat algorithm (KMBA) for efficient clustering.
- Chaotic Bat Algorithm (CBA):(Lin, 2012) presented a chaotic bat algorithm using Levy flights and chaotic maps to carry out parameter estimation in dynamic biological systems.
- Binary bat algorithm (BBA):(Nakamura, 2012) developed a discrete version of bat algorithm to solve classifications and feature selection problems.
- Differential Operator and Levy flights Bat Algorithm (DLBA):(Xie, 2013) presented a variant of bat algorithm using differential operator and Levy flights to solve function optimization problems.

Improved bat algorithm (IBA):(Jamil, 2013)extended the bat algorithm with a good combination of Levy flights and subtle variations of loudness and pulse emission rates. They tested the IBA versus over 70 different test functions and proved to be very efficient.

Applications of bat algorithm

- Bat algorithm and its variants have been applied in almost every area of optimization, classifications, image processing, feature selection, scheduling, data mining and others. For example:
- (Bora, 2012)Optimized the brushless DC wheel motors using batalgorithm with superior results.
- (Yang, X. S., Karamanoglu, M., Fong, S, 2012)Used the bat algorithm to study topological shape optimization in microelectronic applications so that materials of different thermal properties can be placed in such a way that the heat transfer is most efficient under stringent constraints.
- (Jacob, 2014) used Bat algorithm to schedule resources in heterogeneous cloud computing environment with high accurate values as compared to other optimization techniques
- (Abdel-Rahman, E. M., Ahmad, A. R, 2012)Presented a study for full body human pose estimation using bat algorithm, and they concluded that BA performs better than particle swarm optimization (PSO), particle filter (PF) and annealed particle filter (APF).
- (P.R Srivastava, 2014)Proposed a model using the meta-heuristic bat algorithm to estimate the test effort. The proposed model is then used

to optimize the effort by iteratively improving the solutions.

- (Lemma, T. A., Bin Mohd Hashim, F, 2011)Used fuzzy systems and bat algorithm for energy modelling, and later Tamiru and Hashim (2013) applied bat algorithm to study fuzzysystems and to model energy changes in a gas turbine.

(Du, 2012) presented a variant of bat algorithm with mutation for image matching, and they indicated that their bat-based model is more effective and feasible in imagine matching than other models such as differential evolution and genetic algorithms.

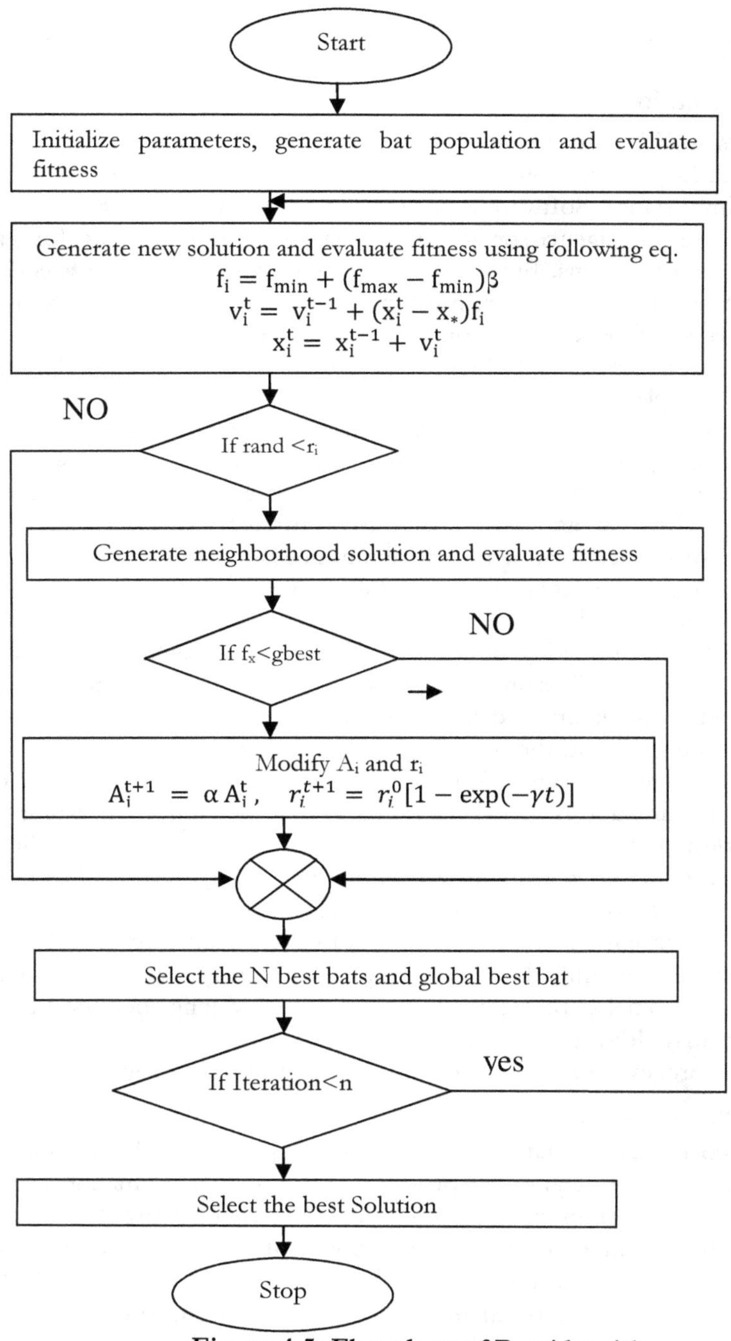

Figure 4.5: Flowchart of Bat Algorithm

Chapter Five: **Software Cost Model and Estimation**

5.1 Introduction

In today's world, software has its own importance which can be seen in every field. Dependency on software is increasing day by day because of its extreme importance. Software is used in various domains either to support the speed or intelligence or to reduce hardware resources or for easy maintenance of systems. But one concern here that needs to be heeded is the software cost. Any software must incur less cost and should be available in the market before any of its competitors can even think of that.

But software cost should be estimated before the project development actually takes place. Estimating proper software cost is very complex and challenging task for every project manager. Software cost is directly proportional to the resources and time required by the project which is dependent on the software attributes and characteristics. As attributes are really very dynamic and are related to a project, so for proper cost estimation prudential treatment of attributes needs to be done.

Estimating future costs and schedule is very much tedious for any analyst. Some of tradition cost estimating techniques include parametric, bottoms-up and estimating by analogy. Here, lies a drawback in all these techniques and i.e. all estimation of cost are based on the relationship constructed with historical data. It assumes that the cost incurred by a model will be similar to the part that has been constructed in past and that is similar to new one. But if future that changes, it will not be of any use unless cost estimation is scaled according to that. Software cost estimation is done during the software development life cycle (SDLC). Initially all resources are identified with their quantity and listed together. Resources used may include list of all software and hardware, testing activities, training session, infrastructure etc. Team members that are needed to complete the project are also identified. After this project manager will estimate the project cost from list of resources that is made. Wrong identification of resources may lead to overbudget and can lead to wrong results in estimation process. So, some tool is required by the manager to properly estimate the software cost.

Over cost and over schedule may lead to project failure. Poor estimated projects lead to termination of projects. Software cost estimation can be defined as a collection of techniques that are used by organizations to estimate proposal bidding, probability estimates and project planning. There are certain reasons that cause difficulty in cost estimation are given below:

- practice needs a significant amount of money to perform it
- process is always performed in a hurry
- Experience is required for making the estimates.

5.2 Cost Estimation Models

There are many software cost estimation models that are developed till now. A prototype is basically needed to consider all the factors and attributes of the project to properly estimate the software cost. It is mandatory as it helps in the overall software management, contract establishment, scheduling, and project planning and resource allocation. All the models that are developed till date can be categorized in either of the following two categories:

- Parametric or Algorithmic models.
- Non-Algorithmic methods.

5.2.1 Algorithmic Models

Algorithmic models use mathematical formulas and do some measurements of project attributes. Some of the examples of algorithmic models are given below:

- Function points
- Putnam
- Slim
- SLOC
- The Doty model
- Price-S model
- Estimacs
- Checkpoint

5.2.2 Non-algorithmic Models

Non-algorithmic models consist of a model that do reasoning, applies logic and uses a large knowledge base. These models are based on the phenomenon of learning by experience or can be said as trail by case studies. These type of models include models like

- Analogy costing
- Expert judgment
- Parkinson model
- Price-to-win
- Bottom-up approach
- Top-down approach
- Delphi
- Machine learning etc.

The main difference lies in both is that algorithmic models use calculations. Here in non-algorithmic model cost is estimated using the Cost Estimating Relationships (CERs) with the help of mathematical algorithms and different logics to establish a cost estimate. Once a model is developed, this approach is very easy to use. It uses physical characteristics like mass, number of inputs, outputs, and volume etc. Detailed information is not needed here. But the disadvantage here can be that its difficult to make the model itself. Accuracy can be one of the other flaws here. Algorithmic models have their importance because they provide a properly defined step by step procedure to provide the final outcome.

5.3 COCOMO:

This is the thoroughly documented model that is used for effort estimation in software process development. It provides the formulae for calculating the time schedule, overall development effort, effort break down by phase and activity, and maintenance effort.

There are three classes of system shown in Figure 5.1 in which modeling process is categorized:

1. Embedded: here main concern is on the tight constraints, changing environment and the unfamiliar surroundings. Real-time software comes under this class example aerospace, medicine, automobiles etc.

2. Organic: this is applicable for projects that are small in respect to project size and team size, and projects that have familiar surroundings and have easy interfaces. These may include data processing systems, small libraries or business systems.

3. Semi-detached: These type of software have mixed characteristics of both embedded and organic software. Examples may include operating systems, inventory management systems and database management systems. (Azath & Wahidabanu, 2012)

Three levels of COCOMO was proposed by the Boehm

1) Basic COCOMO
2) Intermediate COCOMO
3) Detailed COCOMO

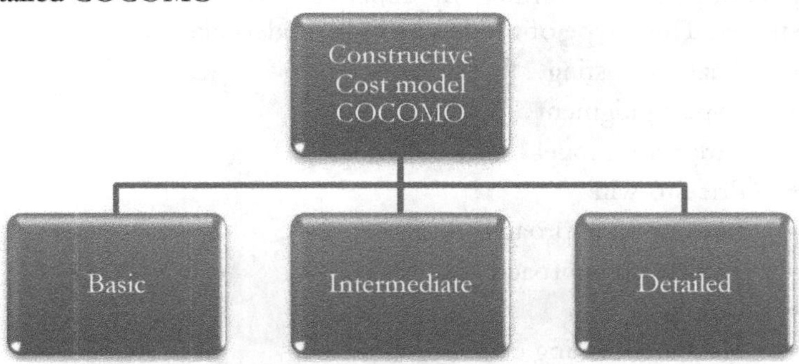

Figure 5.1:Cocomo Model Hierarchy

Majority of software projects apply Basic COCOMO model to estimate the cost of Software Development. What Boehm says about the model is: "Basic COCOMO is good for rough order of magnitude estimates of software costs, but its accuracy is necessarily limited because of its lack of factors to account for differences in hardware constraints, personnel quality and experience, use of modern tools and techniques, and other project attributes known to have a significant influence on costs." (Pandey, 2013)

In Table 5.1 comparison of modes (organic, semi-detached and embedded) in terms of size, nature of project and development environment is illustrated.

Table 5.1: The comparison of three classes of software project

Mode	Project Size	Nature Of Project	Innovation	Deadline of Project	Development Environment
Organic	Typically 2 to 50 KLOC	Small size project, experienced developers in the familiar environment For example : pay roll , inventory projects etc.	Little	Not tight	Familiar and in house.
Semi detached	Typically 50 to 300 KLOC	Medium size project, Medium size team, Average previous experience on similar project. For example: Utility systems like compilers , database systems , editors etc.	Medium	Medium	Medium
Embedded	Typically over 300 KLOC	Large projects, Real time systems complex interfaces. Very little previous experience For example: ATM'S Air Traffic Control etc.	Significant	Tight	Complex Hardware/ customer interfaces required.

- **Basic Model**

Basic COCOMO model takes the form

$$E = a * (KLOC)^b \quad (5\text{-}1)$$

$$D = c * (KLOC)^d \quad (5\text{-}2)$$

Where E is effort applied in Person-Months, and D is the development time in months. The values of coefficients a , b , c and d are given in Table 5.2.

Table 5.2 Basic COCOMO coefficients

Software Project	a	b	c	d
Organic	2.4	1.05	2.5	0.38
Semidetached	3.0	1.12	2.5	0.35
Embedded	3.6	1.20	2.5	0.32

- **Intermediate COCOMO**:

It is a software development effort estimation model that does effort estimation as function of program size. Apart from program size it also considers a set of four cost drivers that include subjective assessment of product, hardware, personnel and project attributes. These cost drivers are

- **Product attributes**
  1. Required software reliability
  2. Size of application database
  3. Complexity of the product
- **Hardware attributes**
  1. Run-time performance constraints
  2. Memory constraints
  3. Volatility of the virtual machine environment
  4. Required turnabout time
- **Personnel attributes**
  1. Analyst capability
  2. Software engineering capability
  3. Applications experience
  4. Virtual machine experience
  5. Programming language experience
- **Project attributes**
  1. Use of software tools
  2. Application of software engineering methods
  3. Required development schedule

Each of the fifteen attributes has a rating on a six-point scale that may range from "very low" to "extra high" (in importance or value). An effort multiplier from the Table 5.3 given below is applied to the rating of the attribute. Finally effort adjustment factor is calculated by taking the product of all effort multipliers which ranges from 0.9 to 1.4.

The Intermediate COCOMO formula now takes the form:

$$E = a * (KLOC)^B * EAF \tag{5-3}$$

$$D = c * (E)^d \tag{5-4}$$

Where E is the effort in person-months, KLoC is the estimated number of thousands of delivered lines of code for the project, and EAF is adjustment factor calculated according to Table 5.3.

Table 5.3: :Value of Effort Adjustment Factors (EAF)

Cost Drivers	Ratings					
	Very Low	Low	Nominal	High	Very High	Extra High
Product attributes						
Required software reliability	0.75	0.88	1.00	1.15	1.40	------
Size of application database	------	0.94	1.00	1.08	1.16	------
Complexity of the product	0.70	0.85	1.00	1.15	1.30	1.65
Hardware attributes						
Run-time performance constraints	------	------	1.00	1.11	1.30	1.66
Memory constraints	------	------	1.00	1.06	1.21	1.56
Volatility of the virtual machine environment	------	0.87	1.00	1.15	1.30	------
Required turnabout time	------	0.87	1.00	1.07	1.15	-----
Personnel attributes						
Analyst capability	1.46	1.19	1.00	0.86	0.71	------
Applications experience	1.29	1.13	1.00	0.91	0.82	------
Software engineer capability	1.42	1.17	1.00	0.86	0.70	------
Virtual machine experience	1.21	1.10	1.00	0.90	------	------
Programming language experience	1.14	1.07	1.00	0.95	------	------
Project attributes						
Application of software engineering methods	1.24	1.10	1.00	0.91	0.82	-----
Use of software tools	1.24	1.10	1.00	0.91	0.83	-----

Table 5.4: Intermediate COCOMO coefficients

PROJECT	A	B	c	D
Organic	3.2	1.05	2.5	0.38
Semidetached	3.0	1.12	2.5	0.35
Embedded	2.8	1.20	2.5	0.32

The coefficient (a and b) are given in Table 5.4

- **Detailed COCOMO**

Detailed COCOMO includes all characteristics of the intermediate version along with the assessment of cost driver's impact on each phase (analysis, design, etc.) of the software development process.

For each cost driver attribute different effort multipliers are used. In this model, the whole software is first divided in different modules and then COCOMO is applied separately in each module to estimate the effort and then sum of effort of al modules is takes to calculate the overall effort. In this model, the effort is calculated as function of lines of code and a set of cost drivers that are given according to each phase of software life cycle.

5.4 COCOMO Models and its Variants

COCOMO can be represented as

$$Effort = a(DLOC)^b \tag{5-5}$$

Where DLOC is the independent variable and Effort is the dependent variable.

Four new models were proposed (Sheta, 2006)(Uysal, 2008) to consider the methodology adopted also in the determination of effort. So, now there are 2 independent parameters DLOC and ME and one is dependent parameter i.e. effort.

5.4.1 COCOMO_model1:

$$Effort = a(LOC)^b + c(ME) \tag{5-6}$$

The model considered ME as linearly related with effort. It had three parameters a, b, c

5.4.2 COCOMO_model2:

$$Effort = a(LOC)^b + c(ME) + d \tag{5-7}$$

It had 4 parameters a, b, c, d

5.4.3 COCOMO_model3:

$$Effort = a(LOC)^b + c(ME)^d + e \tag{5-8}$$

It had 5 parameters a, b, c, d, e

5.4.4 COCOMO_model4

$$Effort = a(LOC)^b + c(ME)^d + e(\ln(ME)) + f(\ln(\text{loc})) + g \tag{5-9}$$

So, there were seven parameters in total.

5.5 Parameter Estimation

We know that some of the cost estimation models are present in the form of used for software cost estimation. There are always some unknown parameters in these functions like a, b, α, β etc. In order to find these parameters we need these estimation equations to fit to some meaningful data. This is known as estimating the parameters or parameter estimation. Mainly used approaches include maximum likelihood estimation technique; least square estimation technique etc. Data is directly given as input into the equations to find the parameters in MLE. In least square method, curve described by the function is given to fit to the data and parameters are estimated. In our research we have used least square method to fit data into the equations of the software cost estimation models.

5.6 Least square error

The maximum likelihood technique determines the parameter values directly which are best feasible and optimal. On the other hand, the least squares estimation method estimate the parameter values by choosing those values which fits a curve in the best way. This technique is the best when the size of the sample is medium or small. Mood (Mood, 1974) describes the theory of curve fitting using LSE as "finding parameter values that minimize the "difference" between the data and the function fitting the data, where the difference is defined as the sum of the squared errors." Another way in which this technique can be used is to directly calculate the difference between the calculated and estimated number of defects and then to minimize the difference between the two so that the results are optimized.

Given the data as, $\{(x_1, y_1), \ldots..(x_N, y_N)\}$, the error associated can be estimated by saying $y = ax + b$ by,

$$E(a,b) = \sum_{n=1}^{N} (y_n - y)^2 \tag{5-10}$$

As it can be seen from the eq. 1.8 it is N times the variance of the data set $\{y_1 - (ax_1 + b), \ldots.., y_n - (ax_N + b)\}$. It does not make much difference whether we consider only the variance or N times of the variance to be the error. It must be noted that the error is taken as the function of two variables. The intention here is to determine or estimate those values of parameters a and b which can minimize the error. In multivariable calculus this requires us to find out the values of (a,b) such that

$$\frac{\partial E}{\partial a} = 0, \frac{\partial E}{\partial b} = 0$$

Chapter Six: **Distance Based Approach**

6.1 Overview of Methodology (Sharma, Garg, & Nag, 2010)

The development of the DBA method begins with defining the optimal state of the overall objective, and specifies the ideally good values of attributes involved in the process. The optimal state of the objective is represented by the optimum model, the OPTIMAL. The vector OP, $(r_1, r_2, ..., r_n)$, is the set of "optimum" simultaneous attributes values. In an n-dimensional space, the vector OP is called the optimal point. For practical purposes, the optimal good value for attributes is defined as the best values which exist within the range of values of attributes. The OPTIMAL, then, is simply the SRM that has all the best values of attributes.

It is very unlikely that a certain SRM has the best values for all attributes. Instead, a variety of alternatives may be used to simulate the optimal state. For this reason, the OPTIMAL is not to be considered as feasible alternatives, but it is used only as reference to which other alternatives are quantitatively compared. The numerical difference resulting from comparison represents the effectiveness of alternatives to achieve the optimal state of the objective function. Hence, here, the decision problem is to find a feasible solution which is as close as possible to the optimal point. The objective function for finding such a solution can be formulated as

$$Minimize\ \delta\{Alt(x), OPTIMAL\}$$

$$Subject\ to\ x \varsigma X$$

where $\{Alt(x)\}$, and δ represent a SRM alternative in the n-dimensional space, and the distance from the optimal point, respectively. Thus the problem, and its solutions depend on the choice of optimal point, OPTIMAL, and the distance metric, δ, used in the model. In two dimensional spaces, this solution function can be illustrated as in Figure 6.1, where H is the feasible region, and the OP is the optimal point.

The DBA method determines the point in the H region which is "the closest" to the optimal point, and is graphically explained in Figure 6.2 for two dimensional cases. Note that the lines $(Alt-OP)_{X1}$, and $(Alt-OP)_{X2}$ are parallel to the X1, and X2 axis respectively. Therefore, $(Alt-OP)_{X1} = |OP_{X1} - Alt_{X1}|$, and $(Alt-OP)_{X2} = |OP_{X2} - Alt_{X2}|$

Based on Pythagoras theorem, in two dimensional space, δ is

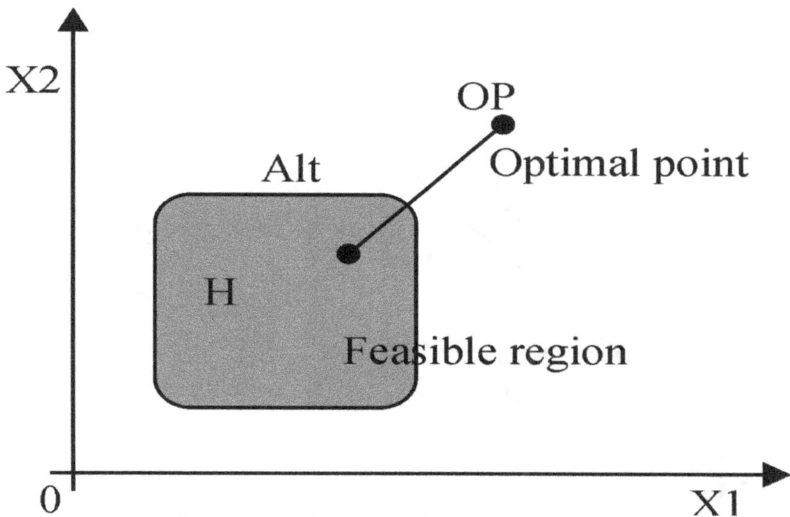

Figure 6.1: Distance Based Approach

$$\delta = \left[(OP_{X1} - Alt_{X1})^2 + (OP_{X2} - Alt_{X2})^2 \right]^{1/2} \tag{6-1}$$

In general terms, the "distance δ" can be formulated as

$$\delta = \left[\sum (OP_{ij} - Alt_{ij})^2 \right]^{1/2} \tag{6-2}$$

where i=1, 2, 3, 4... n = alternative SRMs, and j=1, 2, 3... m = selection attributes.

To implement the above approach, let us assume that we have a complete set of SRMs consisting of 1, 2, 3,...n SRMs, and 1,2,3...m selection attributes corresponding to each alternative SRM, $Alt_1(r_{11}, r_{12}, \ldots, r_{1m})$, $Alt_2(r_{21}, r_{22}, \ldots, r_{2m})$, $Alt_n(r_{n1}, r_{n2}, \ldots, r_{nm})$, and the OPTIMAL $(r_{b1}, r_{b2}, \ldots, r_{bm})$ where r_{bm} = the best value of attribute 'm'. The whole set of alternatives can be represented by the matrix.

$$[r] = \begin{bmatrix} r_{11} & r_{12} & \cdots & r_{1m} \\ r_{21} & r_{22} & \cdots & r_{2m} \\ \vdots & \vdots & \vdots & \vdots \\ r_{n1} & r_{n2} & \cdots & r_{nm} \\ r_{b1} & r_{b2} & \cdots & r_{bm} \end{bmatrix} \tag{6-3}$$

Thus, in this matrix, a vector in an m-dimensional space represents every SRM alternative. To ease the process, and in the same time to eliminate the influence of different units of measurement, the matrix is standardized using

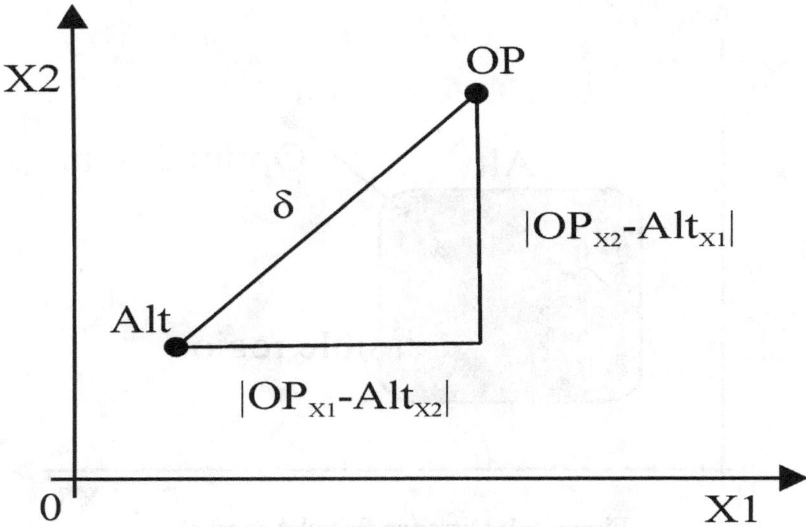

Figure 6.2: Distances of Real Vector

$$Z_{ij} = \frac{r_{ij} - \overline{r}_j}{S_j}$$

Here, $\overline{r}_{ij} = \frac{1}{n}\sum_{i=1}^{n} r_{ij}$, and

$$S_j = \left[\frac{1}{n}\sum_{i=1}^{n}(r_{ij} - \overline{r}_j)^2\right]^{1/2} \qquad (6\text{-}4)$$

where i = 1, 2, 3, ..., n, and j = 1, 2, 3, ... , m.

$\overline{r}_j$, and s_j represent the average value, and the standard deviation of each attribute for all alternative SRMs. m, and n represent the number of different SRM attributes, and the number of alternate SRMs, respectively.

$$\left[Z_{std}\right] = \begin{bmatrix} Z_{11} & Z_{12} & \cdots & Z_{1m} \\ Z_{21} & Z_{22} & \cdots & Z_{2m} \\ \vdots & \vdots & \vdots & \vdots \\ Z_{n1} & Z_{n2} & \cdots & Z_{nm} \\ Z_{OP1} & Z_{OP2} & \cdots & Z_{OPm} \end{bmatrix} \qquad (6\text{-}5)$$

where $Z_{11} = \frac{r_{11} - \overline{r}_1}{S_1}$, $Z_{12} = \frac{r_{12} - \overline{r}_2}{S_2}$, $Z_{1m} = \frac{r_{1m} - \overline{r}_m}{S_m}$.

The next step is to obtain the difference from each alternative to the reference point, the OPTIMAL, by subtracting each element of the optimal set by a corresponding element in the alternative set. This results in another interim matrix

$$[Z_{dis}] = \begin{bmatrix} Z_{OP1} - Z_{11} & Z_{OP2} - Z_{12} & \cdots & Z_{OPm} - Z_{1m} \\ Z_{OP1} - Z_{21} & Z_{OP2} - Z_{22} & \cdots & Z_{OPm} - Z_{2m} \\ \cdots & \cdots & \cdots & \cdots \\ Z_{OP1} - Z_{n1} & Z_{OP2} - Z_{n2} & \cdots & Z_{OPm} - Z_{nm} \end{bmatrix} \tag{6-6}$$

Finally, the Euclidean composite distance, CD, between each alternative SRM to the optimal state, OPTIMAL, is derived from

$$CD_{OP-Alt} = \left[\sum_{j=1}^{m} (Z_{OPj} - Z_{ij})^2 \right]^{1/2} \tag{6-7}$$

Within any given set of SRM's alternatives, this distance of each alternative to every other is obviously a composite distance. In other words, it can be referred to as the mathematical expression of several distances on each attribute in which SRMs can be compared.

6.2 Comparison Criteria

A model can be judged according to its ability to reproduce the observed behavior of the software, and to predict the future behavior of the software from the observed data. To investigate the effectiveness of software cost estimation models, a set of comparison criteria is proposed to compare models quantitatively. The comparison criteria judge the model according to the various properties like fidelity (are the estimated cost close to the actual), stability (does the difference in input is making any difference in output), etc. The comparison criteria we used are described as follows. (Sharma, Garg, & Nag, 2010)

6.2.1 Bias

It can be defined as sum of the difference between the estimated curve, and the actual data. Mathematically, it can be given as (Sharma, Garg, & Nag, 2010)

$$Bias = \frac{\sum_{i=1}^{k} (\text{estimated\_effort}_i - \text{actual\_effort}_i)}{k}$$

Where k represents the sample size of data set.

6.2.2 MSE

The mean square error (MSE) measures the deviation between the predicted values with the actual observations, and is defined as (Sharma, Garg, & Nag, 2010).

$$MSE = \frac{\sum_{i=1}^{k} (actual\_\text{effort}_i - \text{estimated\_effort}_i)^2}{k - p}$$

Where k represents the sample size of the data set and p is number of parameters.

6.2.3 MAE

The mean absolute error (MAE) is similar to MSE, but the way of measuring the deviation is by the use of absolute values. It is defined as (Sharma, Garg, & Nag, 2010).

$$MAE = \frac{\sum_{i=1}^{k} \left| (actual\_effort_i - estimated\_effort_i) \right|}{k - p} \quad (6\text{-}8)$$

Where k represents the sample size of the data set, and p is the number of parameters.

6.2.4 MEOP

The mean error of prediction (MEOP) sums the absolute value of the deviation between the actual data and the estimated curve, and is defined as (Sharma, Garg, & Nag, 2010).

$$MEOP = \left(1 - \left(\frac{\sum_{i=1}^{N} \left| estimated\_effort_i - actual\_effort_i \right|}{k - p + 1} \right) \right) \times 100 \quad (6\text{-}9)$$

Where k represents the sample size of the data set, and p is the number of parameters.

6.2.5 PRR

The predictive-ratio risk (PRR) is defined as (Sharma, Garg, & Nag, 2010)

$$PRR = \sum_{i=1}^{k} \frac{estimated\_effort_i - actual\_effort_i}{estimated\_effort_i} \quad (6\text{-}10)$$

6.2.6 Variance

The variance is defined as (Sharma, Garg, & Nag, 2010).

$$\text{variance} = \sqrt{\frac{1}{k-1} \sum_{i=1}^{k} (\text{actual\_effort}_i \text{-} \text{estimated\_effort}_i \text{-Bias})^2} \quad (6\text{-}11)$$

Where k represents the sample size of the data set.

6.2.7 RMPSE

The Root Mean Square Prediction Error (RMSPE) is a measure of the closeness with which the model predicts the observation. (Sharma, Garg, & Nag, 2010)

$$RMSPE = \sqrt{Variance^2 + Bias^2} \tag{6-12}$$

6.2.8 RSQ

Rsq can measure how successful the fit is in explaining the variation of the data. It is defined as (Sharma, Garg, & Nag, 2010).

$$Rsq = 1 - \frac{\sum_{i=1}^{k}(\text{actual\_effort}_i - \text{estimated\_effort}_i)^2}{\sum_{i=1}^{k}(\text{actual\_effort}_i - \sum_{j=1}^{k}\text{actual\_effort}_j / n)^2} \tag{6-13}$$

6.2.9 SSE

The sum of squared errors (SSE) is defined as (Sharma, Garg, & Nag, 2010).

$$SSE = \sum_{i=1}^{k}(actual\_\text{effort}_i - \text{estimated\_effort}_i)^2 \tag{6-14}$$

6.2.10 TS

The Theil statistic (TS) is the average deviation percentage over all periods with regard to the actual values. The closer Theil's Statistic is to zero, the better the prediction capability of the model. (Sharma, Garg, & Nag, 2010).

$$TS = \sqrt{\frac{\sum_{i=1}^{k}(estimated\_\text{effort}_i - \text{actual\_effort}_i)^2}{\sum_{i=1}^{k}\text{actual\_effort}_i^2}} \times 100\% \tag{6-15}$$

6.2.11 MRE

Magnitude of Relative Error can be defined as (Khalifelua & Ghar, 2011).

$$MRE = \frac{|actual\_\text{effort}_i - estimated\_\text{effort}_i|}{actual\_\text{effort}_i} \tag{6-16}$$

6.2.12 MMRE

The mean magnitude of relative error (MMRE) can be achieved through the summation of MRE over N observations (Satapathy, Kumar, & Rath, 2013).

$$MMRE = \sum_{i=1}^{N} MRE \tag{6-17}$$

6.2.13 RMSE

The root mean square error (RMSE) is just the square root of the mean square error. (Satapathy, Kumar, & Rath, 2013).

$$RMSE = \sqrt{MSE} \tag{6-18}$$

6.2.14 NRMS

The normalized root mean square (NRMS) can be calculated by dividing the RMSE value with standard deviation of the actual effort value for training data set. (Satapathy, Kumar, & Rath, 2013).

$$NRME = \frac{RMSE}{mean(Y)} \tag{6-19}$$

6.2.15 PA

The prediction accuracy (PA) can be calculated as: (Satapathy, Kumar, & Rath, 2013).

$$PA = \left(1 - \left(\frac{\sum_{i=1}^{N} \left| actual\_\text{effort}_i - estimated\_\text{effort}_i \right|}{N}\right)\right) \times 100 \tag{6-20}$$

6.2.16 ED

Euclidian distance (ED) can be defined as (Sheta & Aljahdali, 2013).

$$ED = \sqrt{\sum_{i=1}^{N} (\text{estimated\_effort}_i - \text{actual\_effort}_i)^2} \tag{6-21}$$

6.2.17 MD

Manhattan distance (MD) can be defined as (Sheta & Aljahdali, 2013).

$$MD = \left(\sum_{i=1}^{N} \left| estimated\_\text{effort}_i - actual\_\text{effort}_i) \right|\right) \tag{6-22}$$

6.2.18 SD

Standard Deviation can be defined mathematically as (Foss, Stensrud, & Kitchenh, 2002).

$$SD = \sqrt{\frac{\sum \left(estimated\_\text{effort}_i - actual\_\text{effort}_i \right)^2}{n-1}} \tag{6-23}$$

6.2.19 MdMRE

Median of the Magnitude of Relative Error can be mathematically defined as (Bardsiri, Jawawi b, Bardsiri, & Khatibi, 2013)

$$MdMRE = median(MRE) \tag{6-24}$$

6.3 Model Evaluation

The model must be evaluated in the light of its objectives. The objective is to develop DBA method so that a comprehensive ranking of the alternative cost estimation models could be made combining various attributes relevant to them for a data set. We consider 5 cost estimation models as described in chapter 4 section 4.4 and a dataset has been taken from the open literature for evaluation, optimal selection, and ranking of these five models based on seventeen criteria as described in section 5.2: Bias, MSE, MAE, MEOP, PRR, Variance, RMSPE, Rsq, SSE, TS, ED, PA, SD, MD, MMRE, RMSE, and NRMS. The mathematical form of the five cost estimation models described in equations (4.1) to (4.5) are used to find parameters and to evaluate model selection criteria on the dataset.

For the first time, Bacterial Foraging Optimization (BFO) algorithm is employed along with LSE technique, to calculate values of parameters of these models under discussion for ten datasets. LSE technique is used to get a function of the cost estimation models. This function is called objective function, and is required as an input function to BFOA. The minimized value of objective function is used to find values of parameters. Comparison criteria are computed on these parameters values.

The values of the parameters for these five cost estimation models have been estimated using the LSE technique using BFOA. The estimated values of the parameters have been provided in Table 7.4,Table 7.6 ,Table 7.7 ,Table 7.10 ,**Table 7.12**. The values of the seventeen comparison criteria considered here have been obtained using eq. (6.10) through (6.24). The estimated and optimal values of the model selection criteria are given in Table 7.9.

Matlab7.10.0.499 has been used to model thirteen NHPP SRGMs and to implement BFO algorithm. The values have been computed by matlab programmes executed on intel core 2 duo 2.0 Ghz processor with 4GB RAM under windows 7 environment on matlab 7.10.0.499.

Chapter Seven: **Cost estimation using BAFO**

7.1 Introduction

We have implemented and ranked software Cost estimation models based on Matlab scripting language.

7.1.1 Required Operating Environment

Computers on which Optimal model selection tool will run must have the following characteristics:

1. **Operating Environment** - Microsoft Windows 2000, Windows XP, Windows Vista, or Windows 7.
2. **CPU** – Pentium-IV with an 80387 math coprocessor, Dual core, or Quad core or higher microprocessor based system is recommended.
3. **Disk space** - You should have at least 200 MB of free space on your hard drive to install optimal model selection tool.
4. **Pointing device** - Two-button Windows-compatible mouse. It will not run without a mouse or equivalent pointing device (e.g. Windows-compatible trackball, touch pad, or digitizing tablet).
5. **Memory** - 1GB of RAM is recommended.
6. **Monitor** - A 17" or larger VGA or better quality monitor/TFT/LCD supported by Windows is expected.
7. **Printer** - a printer supported by Windows is assumed. A 300dpi or better resolution laser printer is highly recommended.

7.2 Flow of adopted approach

Procedure adopted to rank the cost estimation models using BFO and DBA is described below:

7.2.1 Step 1: Determination of Parameters of COCOMO model and four of its variants using Bacterial Foraging Algorithm

Input: KLOC, ME, Actual Effort [Table 7.2]

Output: Parameters of all five model and corresponding estimated efforts.

First step is the determination of parameters of COCOMO model and four of its modifications using Bacterial Foraging Algorithm. Bacterium moves in the search space in search of food. It means objective of bacteria is to move to the position with highest nutrient value. Highest nutrient position is considered to be a position with lowest energy. So, overall objective of the algorithm is to find the position with lowest energy. Now, the problem of estimation of parameters of COCOMO and its variants has to be mapped to the bacterial forging optimization problem. For this purpose position of each bacterium is considered as one set of parameter of a particular model. Now, according to algorithm all the bacteria are initialized with some random position. So, set of random position is equal to the number of bacteria. Now iteration of four events of bacterium life cycle will start. Value of p (dimension in BFOA) will be equal to the number of parameters in the model whose parameters are required to be found out. Therefore, it can be observed that number of parameters correspond to the number of dimension in BFO. Table 7.1 shows the value of p for each cost estimation model considered in this research.

Table 7.1:Value of p for each model

Model	p
COCOMO	2
COCOMO_model1	3
COCOMO_model2	4
COCOMO_model3	5
COCOMO_model4	7

- Chemotaxis: Initial energy is calculated. However, process to calculate the energy will change a bit. Now, energy function will be composed of LSE and J. In BFOA for given parameters J value is calculated. Now, LSE is also calculated in addition to J. In addition to J, LSE also need to be minimized. So, fitness function is sum of J and LSE. Rest of the procedure for chemotaxis remains same.

$$J = J_{cc} + LSE$$

$$\begin{aligned} J_{cc}\left(\theta, P(j,k,l)\right) &= \sum_{i=1}^{S} J_{cc}\left(\theta, \theta^{i}(j,k,l)\right) \\ &= \sum_{i=1}^{S}\left[-d_{attractant}\exp\left(-w_{attractant}\sum_{m=1}^{p}\left(\theta_m - \theta_m^i\right)^2\right)\right] \\ &+ \sum_{i=1}^{S}\left[-h_{repellent}\exp\left(-w_{repellent}\sum_{m=1}^{p}\left(\theta_m - \theta_m^i\right)^2\right)\right] \end{aligned} \qquad (7\text{-}1)$$

$$LSE = \sum\left(Estimated\_\text{effort-Actual\_effort}\right)^2$$

Estimated effort is calculated according to the model used. Reproduction and Elimination dispersal steps are carried as described in the original BFOA.

7.2.2 Step 2: Evaluation of Criteria

Input: Estimated Efforts, Actual Effort.
Output: Values determined for criteria.

All the five models are evaluated against the 17 criteria. The criteria that are used are BIAS, MSE, MAE, MEOP, PRR, Variance, RMPSE, RSQ, SSE, TS, MMRE, RMSE, NRMS, PA, ED, MD, and SD. After determination of parameters of all the models, they are evaluated against the criteria stated above.

7.2.3 Step 3: Finally DBA (Distance Based Approach) is applied to rank all the algorithms.

Input: Values determined of criteria
Output: Rank of cost estimation models

7.3 Data Set and Parameters Value Used

Data set that was used is shown in the table below. The data set was given by Bailey and Basili so as to develop the model for effort estimation. Data set in Table 7.2 contains loc in first column i.e. line of code and methodology used in second column of the table as the input. Data for the first 13 projects is used for the purpose of training and other 5 is used for the purpose of testing. Estimated efforts computed with various models are compared with the actual efforts.

Table 7.2:NASA Data Set

LOC	Actual_Efforts	ME
90.2	115.8	30
46.2	96	20
46.5	79	19
54.5	90.8	20
31.1	39.6	35
67.5	98.4	29
12.8	18.9	26
10.5	10.3	34
21.5	28.5	31
3.1	7	26
4.2	9	19
7.8	7.3	31
2.1	5	28
5	8.4	29
78.6	98.7	35
9.7	15.6	27
12.5	23.9	27

100.8	138.3	34

The below results are calculated with the parameters values given in the following Table 7.3:

Table 7.3: Parameters used for BFOA

PARAMETER	VALUE
Number of Bacteria	20
Number of Chemotactic Step	40
Number of Swimming Step	8
Number of Reproduction Step	4
Number of Elimination Dispersal Step	4

7.4 Results obtained

7.4.1.1 Results obtained for COCOMO

Table 7.4 shows the value of two parameters obtained for the COCOMO model. These values of a and b were giving minimum LSE. First column is showing the parameter and second column is showing the value obtained for that parameter.

Table 7.4: : Parameters-COCOMO

Parameter	Value
a	2.4279
b	0.8817

Table 7.5 shows the results of the simulation run of the COCOMO model on the MATLAB. Second column shows the value of LOC which is one of the independent variable. Third column shows the actual effort measured for the NASA data set. Fourth column shows the estimated effort by the COCOMO model. Values of parameter shown in the table above are used to calculate these efforts. LSE of 1227.7128 is obtained for above parameters.

Table 7.5 :Estimated and Actual-COCOMO

loc	actual_efforts	cocomo_estimated
90.2	115.8	128.569
46.2	96	71.27638
46.5	79	71.6843
54.5	90.8	82.45397
31.1	39.6	50.28027
67.5	98.4	99.56987
12.8	18.9	22.9857
10.5	10.3	19.30249

21.5	28.5	36.3113
3.1	7	6.583615
4.2	9	8.604977
7.8	7.3	14.85219
2.1	5	4.670158
5	8.4	10.03489
78.6	98.7	113.8741
9.7	15.6	17.99979
12.5	23.9	22.51004
100.8	138.3	141.8019

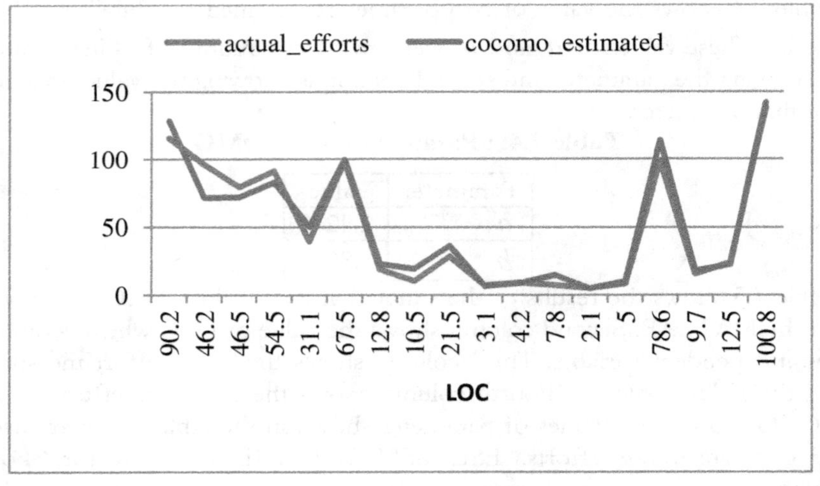

Figure 7.1: Graph for COCOMO

Figure 7.1: Graph for COCOMO shows the graphical representation for the deviation of estimated efforts from the actual effort. Horizontal axis depicts the LOC which was input and vertical axis depicts the Efforts. LSE of 1227.7128 was obtained.

7.4.1.2 Results obtained for COCOMO_MODEL1

Table 7.6 shows the value of two parameters obtained for the COCOMO_model1 model. This value of a, b, and c was giving minimum LSE. First column is showing the parameter and second column is showing the value obtained for that parameter.

Table 7.6: Parameters- COCOMO_model1

Parameter	Value

a	9.9729
b	0.5912
c	-0.7998

Table 7.7shows the results of the simulation run of the COCOMO_model1 on the MATLAB. First column shows the value of LOC which is one of the independent variable. Second column shows the actual effort measured for the NASA data set. Third column corresponds to the value of ME. Fourth column shows the estimated effort by the COCOMO_model1 model. Values of parameter shown in the table above are used to calculate these efforts. LSE of 651.2720 is obtained for above parameters

Table 7.7: Estimated and Actual-COCOMO_model1

loc	actual_efforts	me	cocomo_model1_estimated
90.2	115.8	30	118.8097
46.2	96	20	80.15588
46.5	79	19	81.32432
54.5	90.8	20	90.02187
31.1	39.6	35	48.09942
67.5	98.4	29	97.11694
12.8	18.9	26	24.22505
10.5	10.3	34	12.85183
21.5	28.5	31	36.3791
3.1	7	26	-1.32711
4.2	9	19	8.100073
7.8	7.3	31	8.797576
2.1	5	28	-6.93055
5	8.4	29	2.631526
78.6	98.7	35	103.6492
9.7	15.6	27	16.6175
12.5	23.9	27	22.79842
100.8	138.3	34	125.3059

Figure 7.2 shows the graphical representation for the deviation of estimated efforts from the actual effort for COCOMO_model1. Horizontal axis depicts the LOC which was input and vertical axis depicts the Efforts. LSE of 651.2720 was obtained

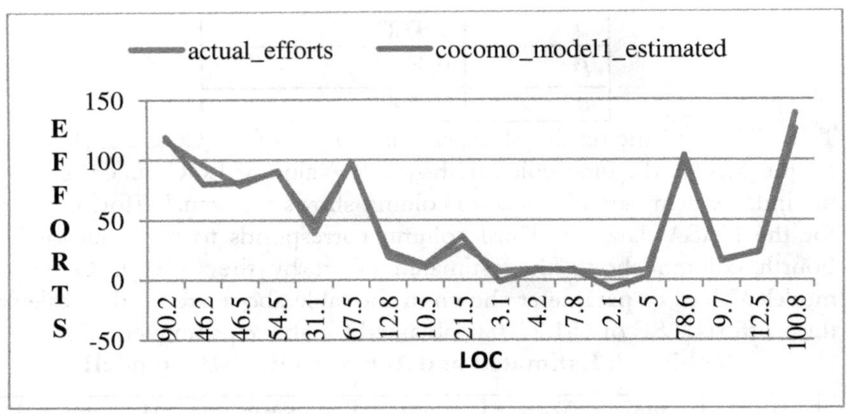

Figure 7.2: Graph for COCOMO_model1

7.4.2 RESULTS OBTAINED FOR COCOMO_model2

Table 7.8 shows the value of two parameters obtained for the COCOMO_model2 model. These value of a, b, c, and d were giving minimum LSE. First column is showing the parameter and second column is showing the value obtained for that parameter.

Table 7.8: Parameters-COCOMO_model2

Parameter	Value
a	6.7987
b	0.6719
c	-1.4746
d	23.5270

Table 7.9shows the results of the simulation run of the COCOMO_model2 on the MATLAB. First column shows the value of LOC which is one of the independent variable. Second column shows the actual effort measured for the NASA data set. Third column corresponds to the value of ME. Fourth column shows the estimated effort by the COCOMO_model2 model. Values of parameter shown in the table above are used to calculate these efforts. LSE of 476.7398 is obtained for above parameters.

Table 7.9: Estimated and Actual- COCOMO_model2

loc	actual_efforts	me	cocomo_model2_estimated
90.2	115.8	30	120.1006
46.2	96	20	81.98924
46.5	79	19	83.78808
54.5	90.8	20	92.56147

31.1	39.6	35	40.26464
67.5	98.4	29	95.66398
12.8	18.9	26	23.94391
10.5	10.3	34	8.437606
21.5	28.5	31	31.47896
3.1	7	26	3.834764
4.2	9	19	16.41172
7.8	7.3	31	7.376208
2.1	5	28	-1.67351
5	8.4	29	4.185275
78.6	98.7	35	100.0845
9.7	15.6	27	16.77257
12.5	23.9	27	21.99422
100.8	138.3	34	125.9551

Figure 7.3 shows the graphical representation for the deviation of estimated efforts from the actual effort for COCOMO_model2. Horizontal axis depicts the LOC which was input and vertical axis depicts the Efforts. LSE of 476.7398 was obtained.

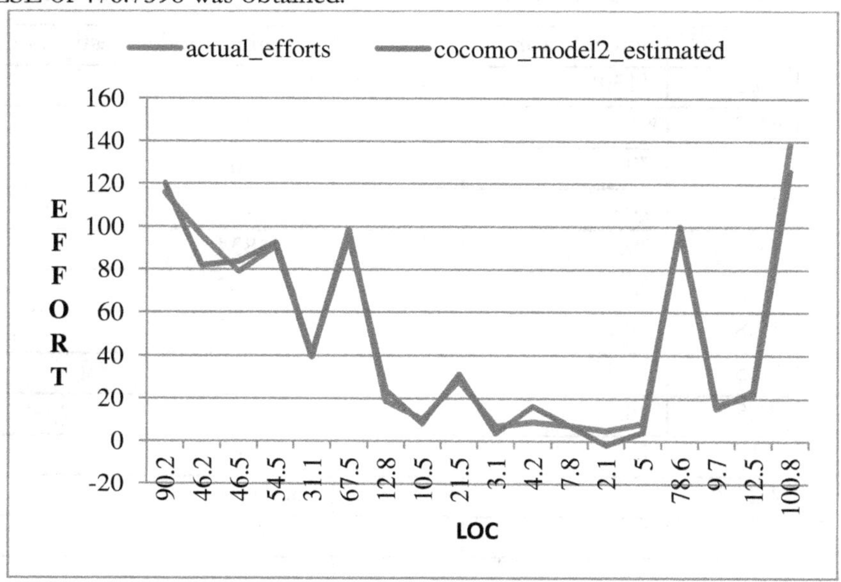

Figure 7.3: Graph for COCOMO_model2

7.4.3 Results obtained for COCOMO_model3

Table 7.10 shows the value of two parameters obtained for the COCOMO_model3 model. These value of a , b , c , d , and e were giving minimum LSE. First column is showing the parameter and second column is showing the value obtained for that parameter.

Table 7.10: Parameters-COCOMO_model3

Parameter	Value
a	7.7960
b	0.6343
c	-0.9401
d	1.0841
e	18.8382

Table 7.11 shows the results of the simulation run of the COCOMO_model3 on the MATLAB. First column shows the value of LOC which is one of the independent variable. Second column shows the actual effort measured for the NASA data set. Third column corresponds to the value of ME. Fourth column shows the estimated effort by the COCOMO_model3 model. Values of parameter shown in the table above are used to calculate these efforts. LSE of 446.1398 is obtained for above parameters.

Table 7.11: Estimated and Actual Efforts-COCOMO_model3

loc	actual_efforts	me	cocomo_model3_estimated
90.2	115.8	30	116.8333
46.2	96	20	83.31446
46.5	79	19	84.9876
54.5	90.8	20	93.11093
31.1	39.6	35	43.44834
67.5	98.4	29	95.42207
12.8	18.9	26	25.97107
10.5	10.3	34	10.48273
21.5	28.5	31	34.51784
3.1	7	26	2.669481
4.2	9	19	15.33051
7.8	7.3	31	8.627129
2.1	5	28	-3.51741
5	8.4	29	4.289172

78.6	98.7	35	98.67209
9.7	15.6	27	18.29254
12.5	23.9	27	24.04201
100.8	138.3	34	121.2743

Figure 7.4 shows the graphical representation for the deviation of estimated efforts from the actual effort for COCOMO_model3. Horizontal axis depicts the LOC which was input and vertical axis depicts the Efforts. LSE of 446.1398 was obtained.

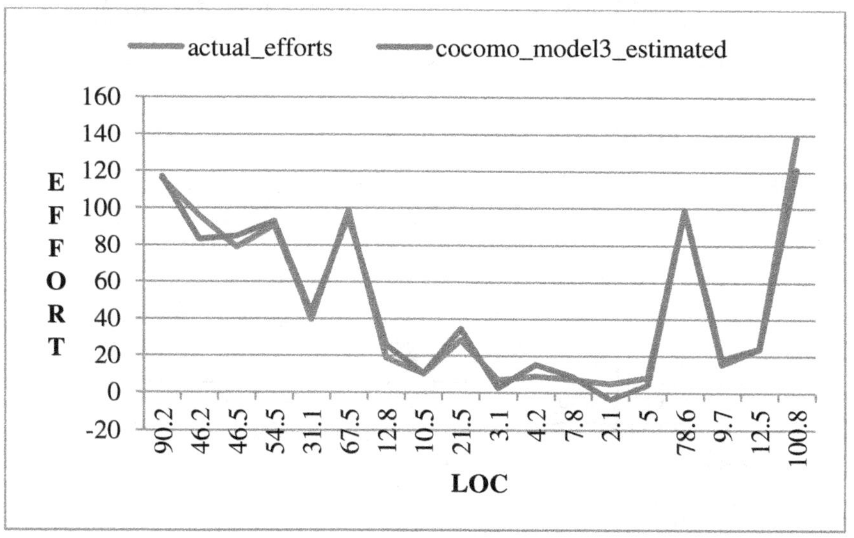

Figure 7.4: Graph for COCOMO_model3

7.4.4 Results obtained for COCOMO_model4

Table 7.13 shows the value of two parameters obtained for the COCOMO_model4 model. These value of a, b, c, d, e, f and g were giving minimum LSE. First column is showing the parameter and second column is showing the value obtained for that parameter.

Table 7.12: Parameters-COCOMO_model4

Parameter	Value
a	4.0933
b	0.7577
c	-1.9088
d	0.9340
e	4.1569
f	1.5473

g	20.7323

Table 7.12 shows the results of the simulation run of the COCOMO_model4 on the MATLAB. Second column shows the value of LOC which is one of the independent variable. Third column shows the actual effort measured for the NASA data set. Fourth column corresponds to the value of ME. Fifth column shows the estimated effort by the COCOMO_model4 model. Values of parameter shown in the table above are used to calculate these efforts. LSE of 451.3753 is obtained for above parameters.

Table 7.13: Estimated and Actual COCOMO_model4

S.No	loc	actual_efforts	me	cocomo_model4_estimated
1	90.2	115.8	30	120.1186
2	46.2	96	20	82.49775
3	46.5	79	19	84.12727
4	54.5	90.8	20	92.71668
5	31.1	39.6	35	43.34774
6	67.5	98.4	29	96.49507
7	12.8	18.9	26	26.44356
8	10.5	10.3	34	11.91825
9	21.5	28.5	31	34.42817
10	3.1	7	26	5.646882
11	4.2	9	19	17.47326
12	7.8	7.3	31	10.42199
13	2.1	5	28	0.01857
14	5	8.4	29	6.753416
15	78.6	98.7	35	101.1766
16	9.7	15.6	27	19.38157
17	12.5	23.9	27	24.62457
18	100.8	138.3	34	126.0314

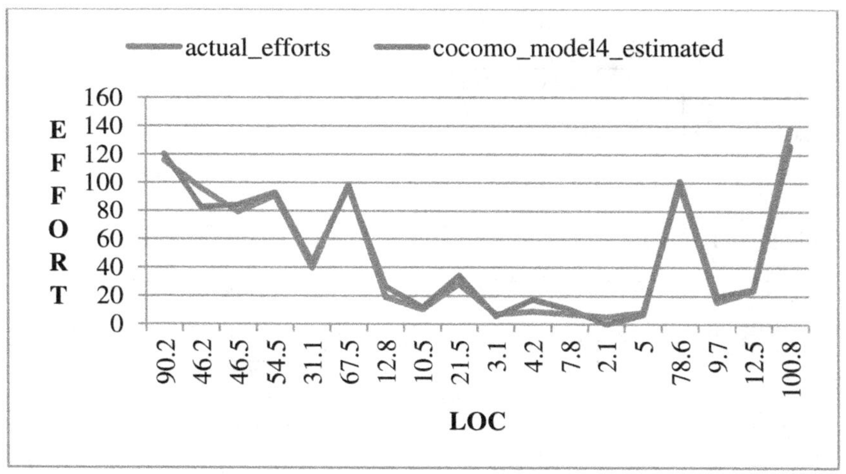

Figure 7.5: Graph for COCOMO_model4

Figure 7.5 shows the graphical representation for the deviation of estimated efforts from the actual effort for COCOMO_model4. Horizontal axis depicts the LOC which was input and vertical axis depicts the Efforts. LSE of 451.3753 was obtained.

7.5 Results obtained after step 2

In the Table 7.14 we have listed all the 5 models in different rows and each column represent one of the 17 criteria discussed in 6.2. For all the models the values for each criterion were obtained by putting outcomes of MVFs i.e. estimated defects and also the observed defects, in the formulas of these criteria. In the last row of the table we can see OPTIMAL value which in this case in the absolute minimum value for each criterion except Rsq for which absolute maximum value is considered. This table is given as the input to the Step 3 of the experimental setup.

7.6 Results obtained after step 3

First step of DBA is to convert the Table 7.15 to Z_{std} table i.e. the standard matrix that can be obtained from eq. 5.8. The structure of the table is same as the above table. This table is the input to find out another intermediate table i.e. Z_{dis} table or the distance matrix which can be obtained from eq.6.6 In the Z_{dis} which has the difference from each alternative to the reference point is the final table that is obtained before composite distance can be calculated. Z_{dis} then serve as the input to find the Euclidean composite distance, between each alternative software cost estimation model to the optimal state. Both the Z_{std} table and Z_{dis} table are shown in Table 7.15 and Table 7.16 respectively.

Table 7.14: Comparison Criteria

Model	BIAS	MSE	MAE	MEOP	PRR	VAR	RMPSE	RSQ
COCOMO	1.8258	92.6266	7.4186	-598.2238	1.3538	9.8877	10.0549	0.9583
COCOMO _model1	-1.2152	58.7022	6.3987	-499.8800	6.4662	7.5158	7.6134	0.9752
COCOMO _model2	-0.9628	40.9368	5.4640	-409.9736	2.5299	6.0545	6.1306	0.9839
COCOMO _model3	-0.7073	58.4837	6.6631	-518.7131	0.8933	6.8053	6.8420	0.9786
COCOMO _model4	0.7290	56.8766	7.6759	-603.6264	-267.1849	6.2041	6.2467	0.9824
Optimal	0.7073	40.9368	5.4640	409.9736	0.8933	6.0545	6.1306	0.9839

Model	SSE	TS	ED	PA	SD	MD	MMRE	RMSE	NRMS
COCOMO	1482.0257	13.6450	38.4971	-559.4336	9.3369	118.6980	-2.6487	9.6243	0.1945
COCOMO _model1	880.5337	10.5176	29.6738	-433.2267	7.1970	95.9808	3.2926	7.6617	0.1549
COCOMO _model2	573.1147	8.4853	23.9398	-324.9780	5.8063	76.4960	1.3837	6.3982	0.1293
COCOMO _model3	760.2884	9.7731	27.5733	-381.2213	6.6875	86.6198	1.2232	7.6475	0.1546
COCOMO _model4	625.6423	8.8656	25.0128	-369.0843	6.0665	84.4352	-1.0148	7.5417	0.1524
Optimal	573.1147	8.4853	23.9398	324.9780	5.8063	76.4960	1.0148	6.3982	0.1293

Table 7.15: Zstd Matrix

Model	BIAS	MSE	MAE	MEOP	PRR	VAR	RMPSE	RSQ
COCOMO	1.6287	1.8391	0.8841	-1.0114	0.4864	1.8588	1.8614	-1.8894
COCOMO _model1	-0.9892	-0.1669	-0.4141	0.3674	0.5338	0.1593	0.1640	-0.0496
COCOMO _model2	-0.7719	-1.2174	-1.6040	1.6278	0.4973	-0.8877	-0.8669	0.8907
COCOMO _model3	-0.5520	-0.1798	-0.0777	0.1033	0.4822	-0.3498	-0.3723	0.3182
COCOMO _model4	0.6844	-0.2749	1.2116	-1.0871	-1.9997	-0.7806	-0.7862	0.7301
Optimum	-0.5520	-0.1669	-0.0777	0.1033	0.4822	0.1593	0.1640	-1.8894

Model	SSE	TS	ED	PA	SD	MD	MMRE	RMSE	NRMS
COCOMO	1.8894	1.8451	1.8451	-1.8080	1.8451	1.8080	-1.5000	1.7800	1.7800
COCOMO _model1	0.0496	0.1418	0.1418	-0.2434	0.1418	0.2434	1.3787	-0.1087	-0.1087
COCOMO _model2	-0.8907	-0.9651	-0.9651	1.0985	-0.9651	-1.0985	0.4538	-1.3246	-1.3246
COCOMO	-	-0.2637	-	0.4012	-0.2637	-0.4012	0.3760	-0.1224	-0.1224

_model3	0.3182		0.2637						
COCOMO _model4	-0.7301	-0.7580	-0.7580	0.5517	-0.7580	-0.5517	-0.7084	-0.2242	-0.2242
Optimum	0.0496	0.1418	0.1418	-0.2434	0.1418	0.2434	0.3760	-0.1087	-0.1087

Table 7.16: Zdis Matrix

Model	BIAS	MSE	MAE	MEOP	PRR	VAR	RMPSE	RSQ
COCOMO	-2.1806	-2.0060	-0.9618	1.1147	-0.0043	-1.6995	-1.6975	0.0000
COCOMO _model1	0.4372	0.0000	0.3365	-0.2640	-0.0516	0.0000	0.0000	-1.8398
COCOMO _model2	0.2199	1.0505	1.5263	-1.5245	-0.0152	1.0470	1.0309	-2.7801
COCOMO _model3	0.0000	0.0129	0.0000	0.0000	0.0000	0.5090	0.5363	-2.2076
COCOMO _model4	-1.2364	0.1080	-1.2893	1.1904	2.4818	0.9398	0.9501	-2.6195
Optimum	-0.5520	-0.1669	-0.0777	0.1033	0.4822	0.1593	0.1640	-1.8894

Model	SSE	TS	ED	PA	SD	MD	MMRE	RMSE	NRMS
COCOMO	-1.8398	-1.7033	-1.7033	1.5645	-1.7033	-1.5645	1.8760	-1.8886	-1.8886
COCOMO _model1	0.0000	0.0000	0.0000	0.0000	0.0000	0.0000	-1.0027	0.0000	0.0000
COCOMO _model2	0.9403	1.1069	1.1069	-1.3419	1.1069	1.3419	-0.0778	1.2160	1.2160
COCOMO _model3	0.3678	0.4055	0.4055	-0.6447	0.4055	0.6447	0.0000	0.0137	0.0137
COCOMO _model4	0.7797	0.8998	0.8998	-0.7951	0.8998	0.7951	1.0844	0.1156	0.1156
Optimum	0.0496	0.1418	0.1418	-0.2434	0.1418	0.2434	0.3760	-0.1087	-0.1087

Once the composite distance value is known we can find out the rank of each model on the basis of this distance with shortest or lowest composite distance being the best is given rank 1 and longest composite distance being the worst is given rank 13 which is the lowest rank in our case. The composite distance and ranks of the models based on the contributing criteria are shown in Table 7.17

Table 7.17: Composite Distance and Ranking of Cost Estimation Models

MODEL NAME	COMPOSITE DISTANCE(CD) VALUE	RANK
COCOMO	6.6599	5
COCOMO_MODEL1	2.1834	1
COCOMO_MODEL2	5.1787	4
COCOMO_MODEL3	2.6231	2
COCOMO_MODEL4	4.9931	3

Chapter Eight: **Optimized COCOMO model with Bat Algorithm**

In this chapter, we describe the proposed methodology by us for optimizing coefficients (a & b) in Intermediate COCOMO Model of Effort estimation (for all types of system i.e. organic, semi-detached and embedded) with Bat Algorithm. We have also given the datasets which have been used.

8.1 Proposed methodology

Bat Algorithm and Intermediate COCOMO Model of effort Estimation have already been discussed in detail in Chapter 5.

Here, we discuss how Bat algorithm is used to find a_best and b_best value for Intermediate COCOMO model (for all types of system i.e. organic, semi-detached and embedded).To derive the new values of coefficients for all types of system (organic, semi-detached and embedded), we have taken NASA 63 dataset and divided it into three sections:

- Dataset for Organic System
- Dataset for Semi-Detached System
- Dataset for Embedded System

Then we have applied Bat Algorithm to each section and calculate new values of a and b for all three types of system (organic, semi-detached and embedded).

8.2 Datasets

Each dataset consist of Project No, its size in KLOC, Effort Adjustment Factor and actual effort for its development.

Dataset for Organic System

Table 8.1: NASA 63 dataset for Organic systems

PROJECT NO.	KLOC	EAF	Actual Effort
1	132	0.320461	243
2	60	0.998141	240
3	16	0.656169	33
4	4	1.865036	43
5	25	0.85243	79
6	9.4	1.657303	88
7	15	0.68887	55
8	60	0.372242	47
9	15	0.358804	12
10	6.2	0.387744	8

11	3	0.964898	8
12	5.3	0.254454	6
13	45.5	0.587344	45
14	28.6	1.069813	83
15	30.6	1.336619	87
16	35	0.872678	106
17	73	0.824729	126
18	24	1.28037	176
19	10	2.304555	122
20	5.3	1.154275	14
21	4.4	0.77736	20
22	25	1.089608	130
23	23	1.006967	70
24	6.7	2.125489	57
25	10	0.386126	15

Dataset for semi-detached system

Table 8.2: NASA 63 Dataset for Semi Detached

PROJECT NO.	KLOC	EAF	Actual Effort
1	293	0.842266296	1600
2	1150	0.675539854	6600
3	77	0.908416597	539
4	13	2.810694546	98
5	2.14	0.994394537	7.3
6	62	3.439167383	1063
7	13	2.178793679	82
8	23	0.380665662	36
9	464	0.758080034	1272
10	8.2	1.376017605	41
11	28	0.446598709	50

Dataset for Embedded system

Table 8.3 :NASA 63 Dataset for Embedded system

PROJECT NO.	SIZE (KLOC)	EFFORT ADJUSTMENT FACTOR (EAF)	Actual Effort
1	113	2.288114989	2040

2	6.9	0.531284635	8
3	22	5.509905793	1075
4	30	2.013772319	423
5	29	1.730150413	321
6	32	1.730150413	218
7	37	0.936262003	201
8	3	4.945017866	60
9	3.9	3.043530256	61
10	6.1	2.374955594	40
11	3.6	1.947463587	9
12	320	3.271167233	11400
13	299	3.487908449	6400
14	252	0.846066335	2455
15	118	0.96815931	724
16	90	0.702502121	453
17	38	1.163900531	523
18	48	0.952487929	387
19	1.98	0.994394537	5.9
20	390	0.569092582	702
21	42	2.301870948	605
22	23	1.476736523	230
23	91	0.301677206	156
24	6.3	0.340097967	18
25	27	2.660867206	958
26	17	3.306315857	237
27	9.1	1.053619034	38

8.3 Model description

The following is the methodology employed to tune the parameters in each proposed modes (organic, semi-detached and imbedded).

Input: Size of Software Projects, Measured Efforts, Effort Adjustment factor-EAF.

Output: Optimized coefficients a_best, b_best and f_{min}(Least MMRE of all projects)

Step 1: Initialize the bat population X_i (i = 1, 2... n) and V_i, where X_i represents the position or solution and V_i represents the velocity of Bats.

Each bat tries to find value for a & b such that MMRE of all project decreases with iteration and after all iterations we get the bat with least MMRE as the best Bat and its values as result.

Step 2: Define pulse frequency f_i at x_i. Thus each bat will have frequency. We have to set F_{min} and F_{max} according to our problem as detectable range should be chosen such that it is comparable to the size of the domain of interest.

Step 3: Initialize pulse rates r_i and the loudness A_i, where (i= 1 to n). The rate of pulse can simply be in the range of [0, 1] where 0 means no pulses at all, and 1 means the maximum rate of pulse emission. For setting loudness we can use A_{max}= 1 and A_{min} = 0, assuming A_{min} = 0 means that a bat has just found the prey and temporarily stop emitting any sound.

Step 4: Repeat the following steps 5 to 9 until number of iterations specified by the user Exhaust.

Step 5: for i = 1, 2... n do // for all the Bats

Step 6: Generate new solutions by adjusting frequency, and updating velocities and locations/solutions

Step 7: For each bat position with values of tuning parameters (a and b), evaluate the fitness function. The fitness function here is Mean Magnitude of Relative Error (MMRE). Thus we are calculating MMRE for each Bat and considering all projects at one time for each bat. The objective in this method is to minimize the MMRE by selecting appropriate values for a and b and then select the least MMRE among all bats as the final result. All Bats fitness is stored in array Fitness (i)

Step 8: if (rand >r_i), then Generate a new solution around the current global best Solution using equation 6.1 and evaluate its Fitness as F_New.

Step 9: If (rand < Ai &&F_New<Fitness (i)) Accept the new solution and update the Fitness (i) =F_New Increase r_i and reduce A_i using

Step 10: Post process the result

Step 11: Stop

The proposed model is implemented in MATLAB for all modes.

8.4 Proposed modes

- **Organic mode with Bat Algorithm:** In this we have taken 25 organic type projects from NASA 63 Dataset and then applied the model described in 3.1.2 to get values a_best, b_best and fmin (Mean Magnitude of Relative Error). In the whole process we are calculating a_best, b_best and fmin (MMRE) for all bats and then taking the least fmin among all bats as global best value and its corresponding best value as final a_best and b_best.

For tuning the parameters, we have taken the values as illustrated in Table **8.4**.

Table 8.4: Parameters value for Organic Mode

Parameter	Value
Dimension (d)	2; (a and b)
F_Min	0
F_Max	4
Lower Bound	0
Upper Bound	4
No. of Iterations	400
No. of Bats	27
Pulse Rate Range	[0,1]
Amplitude Range	[0,1]
Alpha(α)	0.976
Gamma(ϒ)	0.976

8.5 Semi Detached mode with Bat Algorithm:

In this we have taken 11 semi-detached type projects from NASA 63 Dataset and then applied the model described in 3.1.2 to get values a_best, b_best and fmin (Mean Magnitude of Relative Error). In the whole process we are calculating a_best, b_best and fmin (MMRE) for all bats and then taking the least fmin among all bats as global best value and its corresponding best value as final a_best and b_best.

For tuning the parameters, we have taken the values as illustrated in Table 8.5

Table 8.5: Parameters value for Semi-detached Mode

Parameter	Value
Dimension (d)	2; (a and b)
F_Min	0
F_Max	4
Lower Bound	0
Upper Bound	4
No. of Iterations	400
No. of Bats	27
Pulse Rate Range	[0,1]
Amplitude Range	[0,1]
Alpha(α)	0.976
Gamma(ϒ)	0.976

8.6 Embedded mode with Bat Algorithm:

In this we have taken 27 embedded type projects from NASA 63 Dataset and then applied the model described in 3.1.2 to get values a_best, b_best and f_{min} (Mean Magnitude of Relative Error). In the whole process we are calculating a_best, b_best and f_{min} (MMRE) for all bats and then taking the least fmin among all bats as global best value and its corresponding best

value as final a_best and b_best.
For tuning the parameters, we have taken the values as illustrated in Table 3.6.

Table 8.6: Parameters value for Embedded Mode

Parameter	Value
Dimension (d)	2; (a and b)
F_Min	0
F_Max	3
Lower Bound	0
Upper Bound	3
No. of Iterations	400
No. of Bats	27
Pulse Rate Range	[0,1]
Amplitude Range	[0,1]
Alpha(α)	0.976
Gamma(ϒ)	0.976

During the experiments, the initial population of 27 bats was generated. Then the optimization of the COCOMO model coefficients was performed using the proposed algorithm. Based on the fact that each of the three modes of COCOMO model has its own coefficients, experiments were performed using datasets according to each mode. Experiments were performed by changing the Bat algorithm parameters (No. of iterations, No. of Bats, Fmin, Fmax, Lower Bound, Upper Bound, Pulse Rate, Loudness, alpha and gamma). Value used for parameters is already discussed in chapter 3.

8.7 Organic mode experiments

In experiments using organic mode datasets, the best result was achieved using 400 iterations and 27 bats. As a result of algorithm execution, we got different values at each execution and mostly the MMRE with Bat Execution was less than that of COCOMO.

Solution:

MMRE by COCOMO: 0.3720

Fmin (Least Mean Magnitude of Relative Error) by Bat Algorithm: 0.3093

a_best=3.63

b_best=0.916

Figure 8.1 depicts how bats are searching for coefficient a and b in the given range [0-4], while execution and Figure 8.2 depicts MMRE for all 27 bats. Bat no. 1 has got the least MMRE for Organic projects.

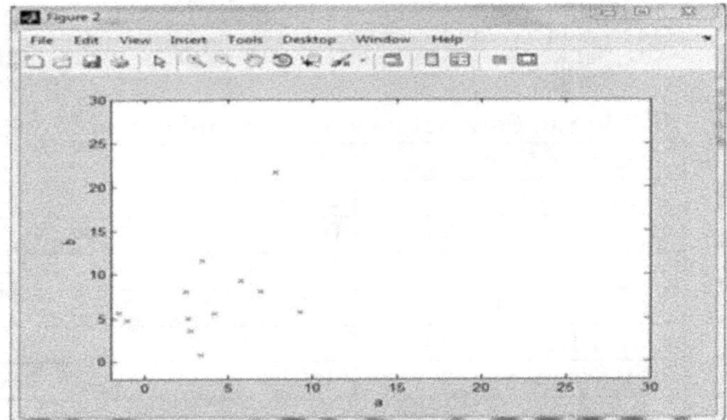

Figure 8.1: Plot of Bats searching for a_best and b_best for Organic Projects

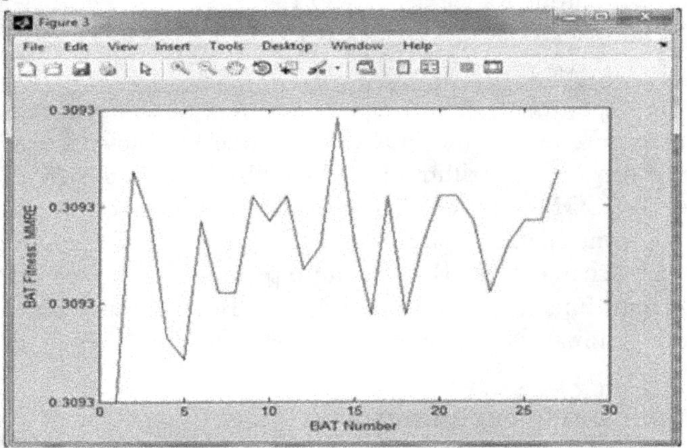

Figure 8.2: MMRE of organic projects for all bats.

Table 8.7 depicts comparison among the organic mode projects real development effort, the predicted development effort using Bat coefficients and the predicted development effort using current COCOMO model coefficients:

Table 8.7: Comparison of MRE of Actual and Proposed Model for Organic Mode

No.	Actual Effort	COCOMO Effort	BAT-COCOMO Effort	MRE (COCOMO-Actual)	MRE(BAT-COCOMO)
1	243	172.79365	101.88905	0.2889150	0.580703482
2	240	235.18016	154.12925	0.0200826	0.357794791
3	33	38.591500	30.192302	0.169439	0.085081734
4	43	25.585869	24.10353	0.4049797	0.439452602
5	79	80.102434	59.030763	0.0139548	0.252775149

6	88	55.76171	46.848280	0.3663441	0.467633176
7	55	37.86021	29.877447	0.3116324	0.456773684
8	47	87.706981	57.48023	0.8661059	0.222983747
9	12	19.719825	15.561931	0.6433188	0.29682761
10	8	8.4276470	7.4865632	0.0534558	0.064179592
11	8	9.7860786	9.5814469	0.2232598	0.197680872
12	6	4.6908216	4.2555196	0.2181963	0.290746719
13	45	103.50336	70.394317	1.3000748	0.564318161
14	83	115.78230	83.800340	0.3949675	0.009642655
15	87	155.29772	111.38714	0.7850313	0.280312039
16	106	116.75499	82.248309	0.1014621	0.22407255
17	126	238.75377	152.41286	0.8948712	0.209625924
18	176	115.26760	85.411355	0.3450704	0.51470821
19	122	82.744103	68.943559	0.3217696	0.434888856
20	14	21.278888	19.304235	0.5199205	0.378873977
21	20	11.786842	10.963051	0.4106578	0.45184741
22	130	102.38993	75.45533	0.2123851	0.41957434
23	70	86.692084	64.604766	0.2384583	0.077074765
24	57	50.117267	44.060559	0.1207496	0.227007731
25	15	13.863695	11.551427	0.0757536	0.229904808
				∑MRE=9.3008 57605	**∑MRE=7.734 484583**
				MMRE:9.30085 7/25 =0.3720	**MMRE:7.7344 8/25= 0.3093**

From Table 8.7 we can draw bar chart as depicted in

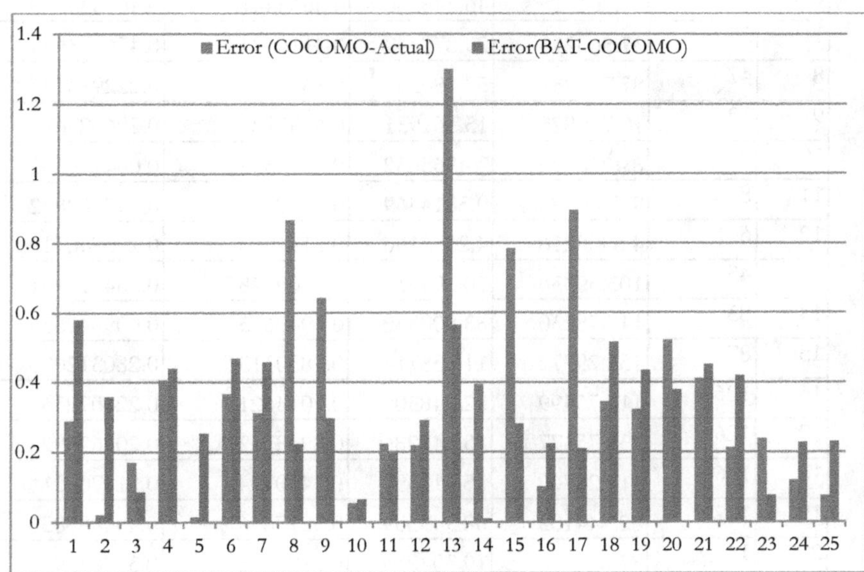

Figure 8.3: Comparison of MRE with COCOMO Model and Proposed Bat Model for all organic projects.

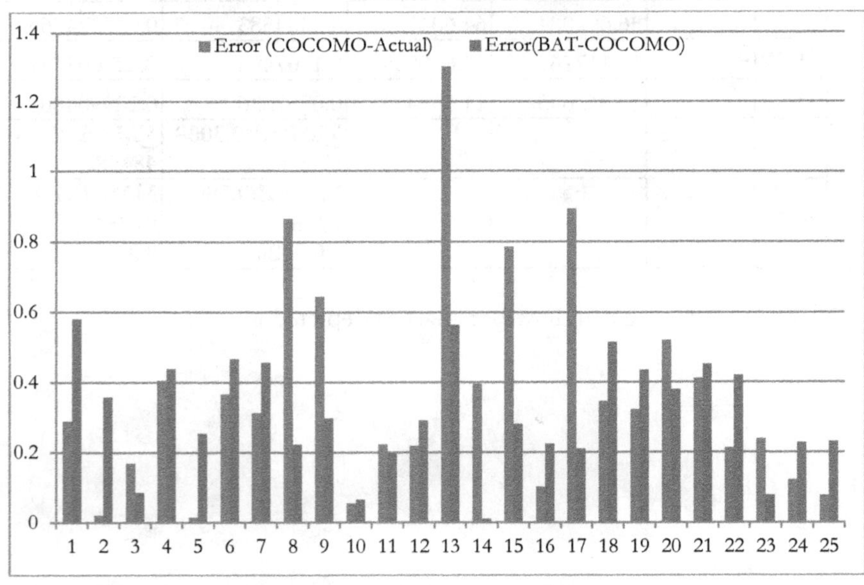

Figure 8.3, which shows comparison of MRE for all organic projects by Actual COCOMO Model and Bat-COCOMO Model.

Results show that MMRE by proposed Bat-COCOMO Model (0.3093) is less than that of Original COCOMO Model (0.3720). From figure we can also see that MRE of most of the projects by proposed Bat-COCOMO Model is less as compared to that of Original COCOMO Model.

8.8 Semi detached mode experiments

In experiments using semi-detached mode datasets, the best result was achieved using 400 iterations and 27 bats. As a result of algorithm execution, we got different values at each execution and mostly the MMRE with Bat Execution was less than that of COCOMO.

Solution:

MMRE by COCOMO: 0.2337

Fmin (Least Mean Magnitude of Relative Error) by Bat Algorithm: 0.2157, a_best=2.9383, b_best=1.1009

Figure 8.4 depicts how bats are searching for coefficient a and b in the given range [0-3], while execution and Figure 8.2 depicts MMRE for all 27 bats. Bat no. 23 has got the least MMRE for semi-detached projects.

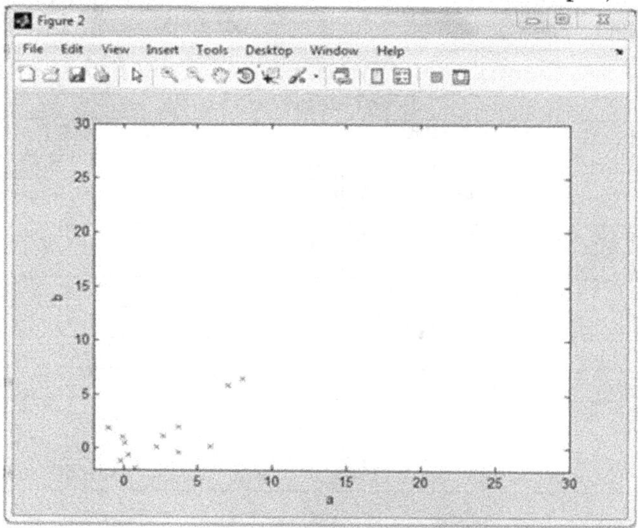

Figure 8.4: Plot of Bats searching for a_best and b_best for semi-detached projects

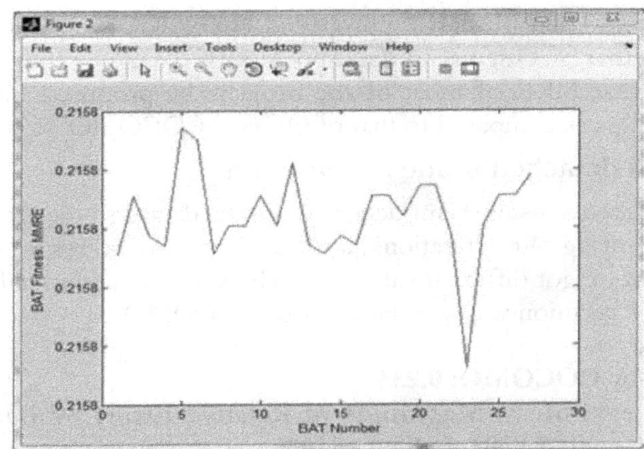

Figure 8.5: MMRE of semi-detached projects for all bats

Table 8.8 depicts comparison among the semi-detached mode projects real development effort, the predicted development effort using Bat coefficients and the predicted development effort using current COCOMO model coefficients.

Table 8.8: Comparison of MRE of Actual and Proposed Model for Semi-detachedMode

No.	Actual Effort	COCOMO Effort	BAT Effort	MRE(COCOMO-Actual)	MRE(Bat-COCOMO)
1	1600	1463.7348	1286.234	0.085165	0.196103
2	6600	5429.4246	4648.034	0.177359	0.295752
3	539	353.4076	318.5802	0.344327	0.408942
4	98	149.1253	139.0753	0.521687	0.419135
5	7.3	6.99428	6.75161	0.041878	0.075121
6	1063	1049.6711	950.1528	0.012538	0.106159
7	82	115.5989	107.8083	0.409743	0.314736
8	36	38.2648	35.2992	0.062912	0.01946
9	1272	2204.6337	1920.351	0.733202	0.509710
10	41	43.57292	40.99565	0.062755	0.000106
11	50	55.957166	51.42684	0.119143	0..28536
				∑MRE= 2.570714	**∑MRE= 2.373768**
				MMRE=2.570714/11 =0.2337	**MMRE=2.373768/11 =0.2157**

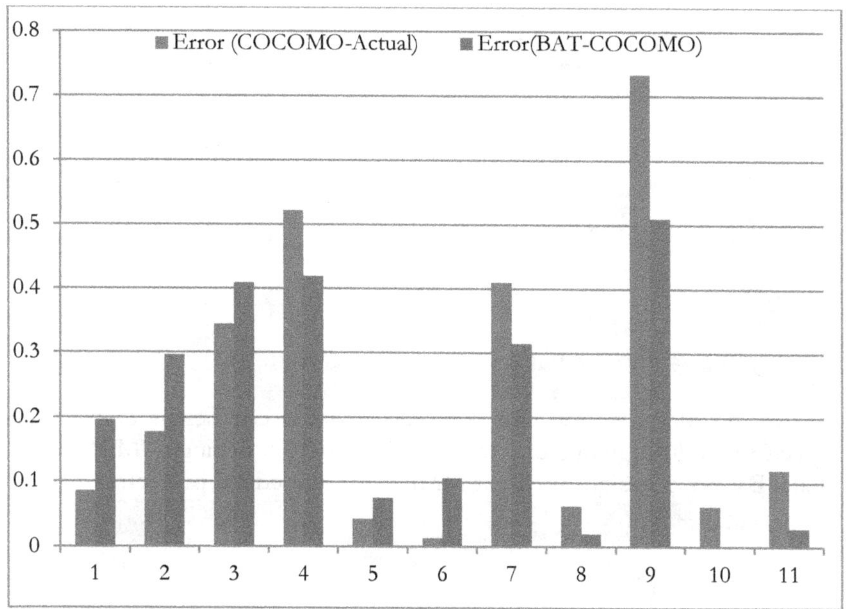

Figure 8.6: Comparison of MRE with COCOMO Model and Proposed Bat Model for all semi-detached projects.

From Table 8.8 we can draw bar chart as depicted in Figure 8.6, which shows comparison of MRE for all semi-detached projects by Actual COCOMO Model and Bat-COCOMO Model.

Results show that MMRE by proposed Bat-COCOMO Model (0.2157) is less than that of Original COCOMO Model (0.2337). From figure we can also see that MRE of most of the projects by proposed Bat-COCOMO Model is less as compared to that of Original COCOMO Model.

8.9 Embedded mode experiments

In experiments using embedded mode datasets, the best result was achieved using 400 iterations and 27 bats. As a result of algorithm execution, we got different values at each execution and mostly the MMRE with Bat Execution was less than that of COCOMO.

Solution:

MMRE by COCOMO: 0.3921

Fmin (Least Mean Magnitude of Relative Error) by Bat Algorithm: 0.3826, a_best=2.8908, b_best=1.1689

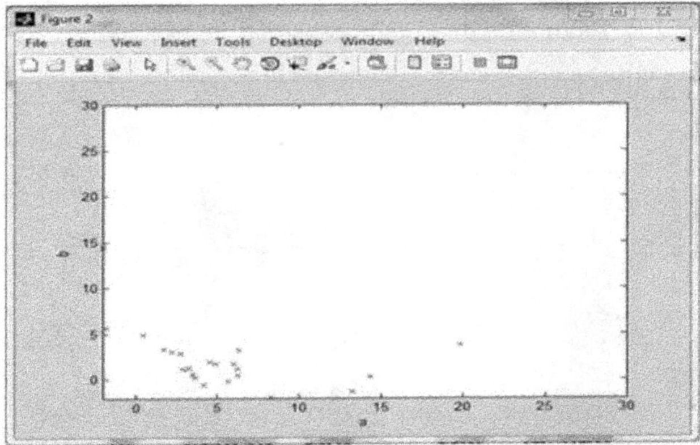

Figure **8.7** depicts how bats are searching for coefficient a and b in the given range [0-3], while execution and Figure 8.8 depicts MMRE for all 27 bats. Bat no. 5 has got the least MMRE for embedded projects.

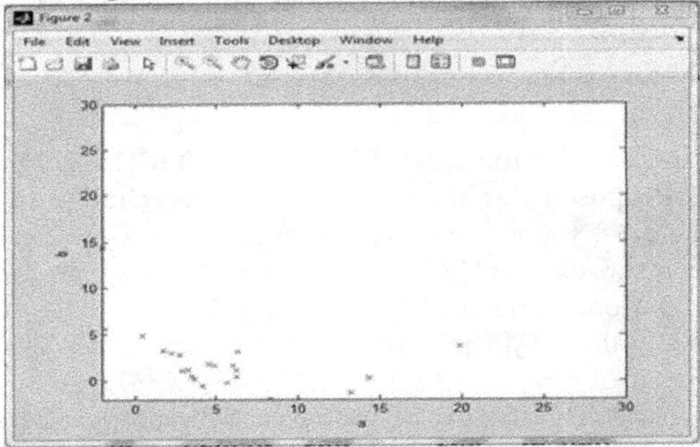

Figure 8.7: Plot of Bats searching for a_best and b_best for embedded projects

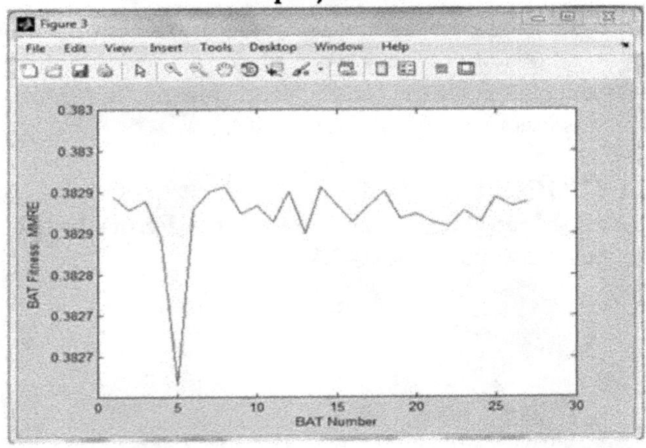

Figure 8.8: MMRE of embedded projects for all bats

Table 8.9 depicts comparison among the embedded mode projects real development effort, the predicted development effort using Bat coefficients and the predicted development effort using current COCOMO model coefficients.

Table 8.9: Comparison of MRE of Actual and Proposed Model for Embedded Mode

NO	Actual Effort	COCOMO Effort	BAT Effort	MRE (COCOMO-Actual)	MRE (BAT-COCOMO)
1	2040	1863.502628	1660.883936	0.086518319	0.185841208
2	8	15.10442497	14.68506943	0.888053122	0.835633679
3	1075	629.8098112	590.6362406	0.414130408	0.450570939
4	423	333.9749579	310.1954673	0.210461092	0.266677382
5	321	275.4986592	256.1526933	0.141748725	0.202016532
6	218	310.042954	287.3900424	0.422215385	0.318302947
7	201	199.7089364	184.2834948	0.006423202	0.083166692
8	60	51.74535872	51.62890875	0.137577355	0.139518188
9	61	43.63281003	43.18084022	0.284708032	0.292117373
10	40	58.23838554	56.83888946	0.455959638	0.420972237
11	9	25.36240179	25.16224492	1.818044644	1.795804991
12	11400	9290.535617	8016.607173	0.185040735	0.296788844
13	6400	9131.214279	7895.782472	0.426752231	0.233716011
14	2455	1804.027257	1568.265371	0.265162013	0.361195368
15	724	830.5451876	739.2439015	0.147161861	0.021055113
16	453	435.4082789	390.822677	0.038833821	0.137256784
17	523	256.3387213	236.3431168	0.509868602	0.548101115
18	387	277.6559578	254.1443206	0.282542745	0.343296329
19	5.9	6.319969602	6.387761855	0.071181288	0.082671501
20	702	2049.361082	1757.504274	1.91931778	1.503567342
21	605	571.6604562	525.4302996	0.055106684	0.131520166
22	230	178.046914	166.7418938	0.225882983	0.275035245
23	156	189.4742512	170.0137422	0.214578533	0.089831681
2	18	8.669034405	8.452228904	0.518386978	0.530431728
25	958	388.8819174	362.37844	0.59406898	0.621734405
26	237	277.3582427	262.2008711	0.170287944	0.10633279

27	38	41.75334845	40.24622374	0.098772328	0.059111151
				∑MRE=10.5887	**∑MRE=10.33226**
				MMRE:10.58878/27=0.3921	**MMRE:10.332267/27=0.3826**

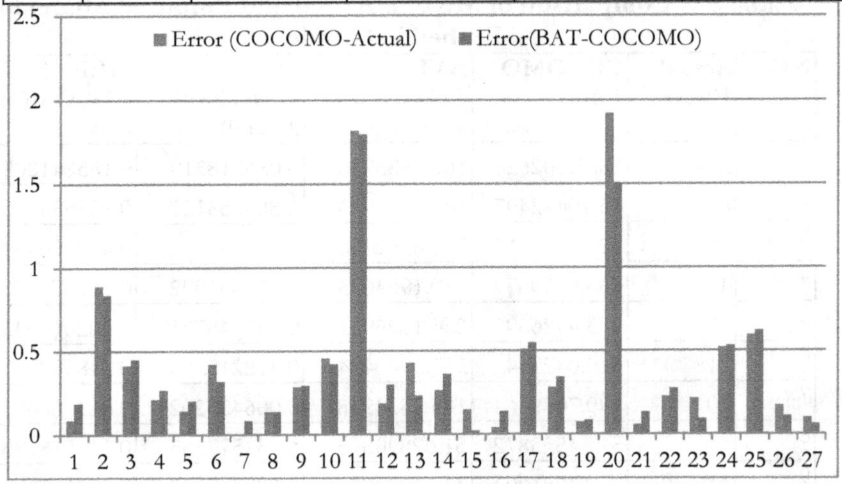

Figure 8.9: Comparison of MRE with COCOMO Model and Proposed Bat Model for all embedded projects

From Table 8.9 we can draw bar chart as depicted in Figure 8.9, which shows comparison of MRE for all embedded projects by Actual COCOMO Model and Bat-COCOMO Model.

Results show that MMRE by proposed Bat-COCOMO Model (0.3826) is less than that of Original COCOMO Model (0.3921). From Figure 8.9 we can also see that MRE of most of the projects by proposed Bat-COCOMO Model is less as compared to that of Original COCOMO Model.

From the above Table 7.17 we can conclude that the COCOMO_model1 is ranked as number one or the best based on the analysis which was done using the 17 criteria and DBA. After that COCOMO_model3 and COCOMO_model4 are ranked. COCOMO and COCOMO_model2 has highest composite distance i.e. five and four respectively.

Parameters of BFOA can be studied in more detail. There are many parameters that are used in the BFOA algorithm. Effects of modifying these parameters can be analyzed. BFOA algorithm can be hybridized with various algorithms like Ant Colony Optimization, Particle Swarm Optimization, Genetic Algorithm, Artificial Bee Colony, Bat Algorithm so as to improve the convergence speed, accuracy of the algorithm. BFOA can be modified in order to mimic the exact natural process of E. Coli bacteria.

For example population of bacteria can be kept variable; all bacteria may not undergo steps like chemotaxis, reproduction, elimination-dispersal at the same time etc. BFOA can be converted be parallel algorithm i.e. it can be parallelized. This will improve the speed of convergence of algorithm because computations can be performed in parallel. Algorithm can also be converted to the Map Reduce form using Hadoop framework so as to handle the big data. Modifications of the BFOA for example Improved BFOA, Self Adapting BFOA, Hybridized BFOA can be applied to estimate the cost so as to obtain better results. BFOA can be applied to other engineering domains as well.

8.10 Future work:

1. A lot of work can be done in Software Engineering using Bat algorithm.
2. We can use Bat Algorithm to optimize other software effort estimation technique such as Function Point Analysis, Use case points or COCOMO II model parameters.
3. We can compare the results of BAT-COCOMO optimization with other new optimization algorithms (PSO, Genetic Algorithm, Firefly Algorithm, Ant Colony Optimization)etc.
4. We can use Bat Algorithm on our own datasets, to get a new model.
5. We can use Bat Algorithm in other software Engineering domains such as Software reliability, Testing etc.

REFERENCES

"The Nature of Mathematical Programming. (n.d.).

Abdel-Rahman, E. M., Ahmad, A. R. (2012). A metaheurisic bat inspired algorithm for full body human pose estimation. *Ninth Conference on Computer and Robot Vision*, (pp. 369–375).

Abraham A., C. G. (2006). Stigmergic Optimization. *Springer*.

Afif Wan, W. N., Rahman, T. K., & Zakaria, Z. (2013). Bacterial Foraging Optimization Algorithm For Load Shedding. *Power Engineering and Optimization Conference (PEOCO), 2013 IEEE 7th International Conference* (pp. 722-726). Langkawi: IEEE.

Albrecht, A. (1979). Measuring Application Development Productivity. *In Proc of the IBM Applications Development Symposium* , (pp. 83-92).

Anish M, Kamal P and Harish M. (2010). Software Cost Estimation using Fuzzy logic. *ACM SIGSOFT Software Engineering Notes*, 1-7.

Anna Galinina, Olga Burceva, Sergei Parshutin. (2012). The Optimization of COCOMO Model Coefficients Using Genetic Algorithms. *Information Technology and Management Science*, 45-52.

Atasagun, Y., & Kara, Y. (2013). Assembly Line Balancing Using Bacterial Foraging Optimization Algorthm. *25*, pp. 237-250. Springer London. doi:10.1007/s00521-013-1477-9

Attarzadeh, I., & Ow, S. H. (2010). A Novel Soft Computing Model to Increase the Accuracy of Software Development Cost Estimation. (pp. 603-607). Singapore: IEEE.

Attarzadeh, I., Mehranzadeh, A., & Barati, A. (2012). Proposing an Enhanced Artificial Neural Network Prediction Model to Improve the Accuracy in Software Effort Estimation. (pp. 167-172). IEEE.

Azath, H., & Wahidabanu, R. D. (2012). Efficient effort estimation system viz. function points and quality assurance coverage. *IET Softwares, 6*(4), 335-341.

Banks A., J. V. (2007). A Review of Particle Swarm Optimization- Part I: Background and Development, Natural Computation. *springer*, 467–484.

Bardsiri, V. K., Jawawi b, D. N., Bardsiri, A. K., & Khatibi, E. (2013). LMES: A localized multi-estimator model to estimate software development effort., (pp. 2624-2660).

Basili, J. B. (1981). A meta model for software development resource expenditures. *Fifth International conference on software Engineering*, (pp. 107-129).

Bejinariu, S. I. (2013). Image Registration using Bacterial Foraging Optimization Algorithm on Multi-core Processors. *Electrical and Electronics Engineering (ISEEE), 2013 4th International Symposium* (pp. 1-6). Galati: IEEE.

Benala, T. R., Chinnababu, K., Mall, R., & Dehuri, S. (2013). A Particle Swarm Optimized Functional Link Artificial Neural Network (PSO-FLANN) in Software Cost Estimation. (pp. 59-66). Springer-Verlag Berlin Heidelberg.

Benala, T. R., Mall, R., Srikavya, P., & HariPriya, M. V. (2014). Software Effort Estimation Using Data Mining Techniques. *1*, pp. 85-92. Springer International Publishing Switzerland.

Boehm., B. (1981). *Software Engineering Economics*. New Jersey.

Bora, T. C. (2012). Bat-inspired optimization approach for the brushless DC wheel motor problem. *IEEE Trans. Magnetics*, 947-950.

Brajesh Kumar Singh, S. T. (2013). Tuning of Cost Drivers by Significance Occurrences and Their Calibration with Novel Software Effort Estimation Method. *Advances in Software Engineering.*

C.F, K. (1996). An Empirical Validation of Software Cost Estimation Models. *ACM*, 416-429.

Chandrasekaran, M., Muralidhar, M., Krishna, C. M., & Dixit, U. S. (2009). Appication of Soft Computing Technique in Machining Performance Prediction and Optimization:A Literature Review. *Springer-Verlag London Limited*, 445-464.

Chen, H., Zhu, Y., & Hu, K. (2008). Self-Adaptation in Bacterial Foraging Optimization Algorithm. *Intelligent System and Knowledge Engineering, 2008. ISKE 2008. 3rd International Conference. 1*, pp. 1026-1031. IEEE.

Chen, Y., & Lin, W. (2009). An Improved Bacterial Foraging Optimization. (pp. 2057-2062). IEEE.

Das, S., Biswas, A., Dasgupta, S., & Abraham, A. (2009). Bacterial Foraging Optimization Algorithm:Theoretical Foundations, Analysis, and Applications. In S. Das, A. Biswas, S. Dasgupta, A. Abraham, A. Abraham, A. E. Hassanien, P. Siarry, & A. Engelbrecht (Eds.), *Foundations of Computational Intelligence Volume 3* (Vol. 3, pp. 23-55). Springer Berlin Heidelberg.

Dolado, J. J. (2009). *On the Problem of the Software Cost Function,*. spain.

Du, Z. Y. (2012). Image matching using a bat algorithm with mutation. *Applied Mechanics and Materials*, 88-93.

F. Ferrucci, C. G. (2010). Genetic programming for effort estimation: an analysis of the impact of different fitness functions. *in Proceedings of the 2nd International Symposium on Search Based Software Engineering (SSBSE '10),* (pp. 89-98). IEEE Computer Society.

Facts about COCOMO And Costar. (2012). Retrieved from http://www.softstarsystems.com/.

Five reason why software projects fail. (2002, may 20). Retrieved from Computerworld.

Foss, T., Stensrud, E., & Kitchenh, B. (2002). A Simulation Study of the Model Evaluation Criterion MMRE., (pp. 1-30).

Hari, C. M., & Sethi, T. S. (2011). CPN-A Hybrid Model for Software Cost Estimation. (pp. 902-906). IEEE.

Hossain, M. A., & Ferdous, I. (2014). Electrical Information and Communication Technology (EICT), 2013 International Conference. (pp. 1-6). Khulna: IEEE.

Huang, W., & Lin, W. (2010). Parameter Estimation of Wiener Model Based on Improved Bacterial Foraging Optimization. *Artificial Intelligence and Computational Intelligence (AICI). 1*, pp. 174-178. Sanya: IEEE.

Jacob, L. (2014). Bat Algorithm for resource scheduling in cloud computing enviornment. *International Journal for research in applied sciences and engineering technology.*

Jamil, M. Z.-J. (2013). Improved bat algorithm for global optimization. *Applied Soft Computing.*

Kashyap a, D., & Misra, A. K. (2014). Software Cost Estimation Using Similarity Difference Between Software Attributes. *Proceedings of the Second International Conference on Soft Computing 1205* (pp. 1205-1215). Springer India.

Kaushik, A., Chauhan, A., Mittal, D., & Gupta, S. (2012). COCOMO Estimates Using Neural Networks., (pp. 22-28).

Kaushik, A., Soni, A. K., & Soni, R. (2012). An Adaptive Learning Approach to Software Cost Estimation. IEEE.

Khalifelua, Z. A., & Ghar, F. S. (2011). Comparison and evaluation of data mining techniques with algorithmic models in software cost estimation. (pp. 65-71). Elsevier Ltd.

Khalifelua, Z. A., & Ghar, F. S. (2012). Comparison and evaluation of data mining techniques with algorithmic models in software cost estimation. (pp. 65-71). Elsevier Ltd.

Khan, K. N. (2011). A fuzzy bat clustering method for er-gonomic screening of office workplaces,. *Advances in Intelligent and Soft Computing*, 59–66.

Komarasamy, G. a. (2012). An optimized K-means clustering techniqueusing bat algorithm. *European J. Scientific Research*, 263-273.

Kotb, M. T., Haddara, M., & Ko, Y. T. (2011). Back-Propagation Artificial Neural Network for ERP Adoption Cost Estimation. (pp. 180-187). IEEE.

Krishnakumar, N., Venugopalan, R., & Rajasekar, N. (2013). Bacterial Foraging Algorithm Based Parameter Estimation of Solar PV Model. *Emerging Research Areas and 2013 International Conference on Microelectronics, Communications and Renewable Energy (AICERA/ICMiCR), 2013 Annual International Conference* (pp. 1-6). Kanjirapally: IEEE.

Kumar, J. S., & Rao, T. G. (2011). A Novel Model for Software Effort Estimation Using Exponential Regression as Firing Interval in Fuzzy Logic. (pp. 118-127). IEEE.

Lemma, T. A., Bin Mohd Hashim, F. (2011). Use of fuzzy systems and bat algorithm for exergy modelling in a gas turbine generator,. *IEEE Colloquium*, 305–310.

Lin, J. H. (2012). A chaotic Levy flight bat algorithm for parameter estimation in nonlinear dynamic biological systems. *J.Computer and Information Technology*, 56–63.

Lin, J.-C. (2010). Applying Particle Swarm Optimization to Estimate Software Effort by Multiple Factors Software Project Clustering. *IEEE.*

Long, L. X., Jun, L. R., & Ping, Y. (2010). A Bacterial Foraging Global Optimization Algorithm Based On the Particle Swarm Optimization. *Intelligent Computing and Intelligent Systems (ICIS), 2010 IEEE International Conference. 2*, pp. 22-27. IEEE.

Lu, Y. f., & Yin, Y. f. (2013). A New Constructive Cost Model for Software Testing Project Management. *The 19th International Conference on Industrial Engineering*, (pp. 545-556).

M.jorgensen, K. a. (2003). A review of software surveys on software effort estimation. *International symposium on Empirical Software Engineering*, (pp. 223-230).

Mansor, Z., & Kasirun, Z. M. (n.d.). Current Practices of Software Cost Estimation Technique in Malaysia Context. (pp. 566-574). Springer Berlin Heidelberg.

Mansor, Z., Yahya, S., & Hj Arshad, N. H. (2011). Success Factors in Cost Estimation for Software Development Project. (pp. 210-216). Springer Berlin Heidelberg.

Michalewicz. (1992). Genetic Algorithms + Data Structures = Evolution Programs. *Springer.*

Mishra, S. (2005). A Hybrid Least Square-Fuzzy Bacterial Foraging Strategy for Harmonic Estimation. *Evolutionary Computation, IEEE Transactions on. 9*, pp. 61-73. IEEE.

Mishra, S. (2005). A Hybrid Least Square-Fuzzy Bacterial Foraging Strategy for Harmonic Estimation. *Evolutionary Computation, IEEE Transactions. 9*, pp. 61-73. IEEE.

Molokken, K. F. (2007). Increasing Software Effort Estimation Accuracy- using experiance data, estimation models and checklists. *&th International conference on Quality Software*, (pp. 342-347). portland.

Mood, A. F. (1974). *Introduction to the Theory of Statistics.* McGraw-Hill.

Nakamura, R. Y. (2012). A binary bat algorithm for feature selection. *25th SIBGRAPI Conference on Graphics, Patterns and Images (SIBGRAPI)* (pp. 291-297). IEEE Publication.

P.R Srivastava, A. B. (2014). An empirical study of test effort estimation based on bat algorithm. *Int. J. Bio-Inspired Computation*, 57-70.

Pandey, P. (2013). Analysis Of the Techniques for Software Cost Estimation. *Third International Conference on Advanced Computing & Communication Technologies.* IEEE.

Passino, K. (2002). Biomimicry of Bacterial Foraging for Distributed Optimization and Control. *IEEE, Control Systems, 22*(3), 52 - 67.

Passino, K. M. (2002). Biomimicry of Bacterial Foraging. *IEEE*, 52-67.

Pattnaik, ,. S., Bakwad, K. M., Devi, S., & Panig, B. K. (2011). Parallel Bacterial Foraging Optimization., *8*, pp. 487-502.

Putnam, L. (1978). A general Empirical Solution to the Macro Software Sizing and Estimating Problem. *IEEE Transactions on Software Engineering* , (pp. 345-360).

Q. Alam, P. (n.d.). Systematic Review of Effort Estimation and cost Estimation. Roorkee: Institute of management studies.

Rao, G. S., Krishna, C. P., & Rao, K. R. (2014). Multi Objective Particle Swarm Optimization for Software Cost Estimation. *1*, pp. 125-132. Springer International Publishing Switzerland.

Reddy, P. (2010). Software effort estimation using Particle Swarm Optimization with inertia weight. *International journal of software Engineering* , 12-23.

Reddy, P. P., & Hari, C. K. (2011). Fuzzy Based PSO for Software Effort Estimation. (pp. 227-232). Springer-Verlag Berlin Heidelberg.

Roy, A. R., & Maji, P. K. (2002). An application of soft sets in a decision making problem. *An international journal computer and mathematics with applications, 44*(8-9), 1077-1083.

S K Sehra, Y. S. (2011). Soft computing techniques for software project effort estimation. *'International Journal of Advanced Computer and Mathematical Sciences*, 160-167.

Satapathy, S. M., Kumar, M., & Rath, S. K. (2013). Fuzzy-class point approach for software effort estimation using various adaptive regression methods. CSI.

Satapathy, S. M., Kumar, M., & Rath, S. K. (2013). Fuzzy-class point approach for software effort estimation using various adaptive regression methods. (pp. 367-380). CSI.

Segundo. (2001). SEER-SEM Users Manual .

Sharma, K., Garg, R., & Nag, C. K. (2010). Selection of Optimal Software Reliability Growth Models Using a Distance Based Approach. *59*, pp. 266-275. IEEE.

Sharma, V., Pattnaik, S. S., & Garg, T. (2012). A Review of Bacterial Foraging Optimization and Its Applications. *National Conference on Future Aspects of Artificial intelligence in Industrial Automation* (pp. 9-12). Proceedings published by International Journal of Computer Applications® (IJCA).

Shepperd, M. J. (2007). A Systematic Review of Software Development Cost Estimation Studies. *IEEE Transactions on Software Engineering.*

Sheta, A. F. (2006). Estimation of the COCOMO Model Parameters Using Genetic Algorithms. *Journal of Computer Science, 2*(2), 118-123.

Sheta, A. F. (2006). Estimation of the COCOMO Model Parameters Using Genetic Algorithms. *Journal of Computer Science, 2*(2), 118-123.

Sheta, A. F., & Aljahdali, S. (2013). Software Effort Estimation Inspired by COCOMO and FP Models: A Fuzzy Logic Approach., *4*, pp. 192-197.

sheta, F. (2006). Estimation of the COCOMO model parameters using genetic algorithms for NASA software projects. *Journal of computer science*, 118-123.

Sheta, S. A. (2007). Software Effort Estimation by Tuning COOCMO Model Parameters Using Differential Evolution. *IEEE congess on evolutionary computation*, 1283-1289.

(2009). *The 10 laws of chaos.* The Standish group International, Inc.

Uysal, M. (2008). Estimation of the Effort Component of the Software Projects Using Simulated Annealing Algorithm., (pp. 258-261).

Vishali, Anshu Sharma, Suchika Malik. (2014). COCOMO model Coefficients Optimization Using GA and ACO. *International Journal of Advanced Research in Computer Science and Software Engineering*, 771-776.

Wu, C., Zhang, N., Jiang, J., Jinhui, Y., & Liang, Y. (2007). Improved Bacterial Foraging Algorithms and Their Applications to Job Shop Scheduling Problems. *Springer-Verlag Berlin Heidelberg*, (pp. 562-569).

X.S., Y. (2008). *Nature-Inspired Metaheuristic Algorithms.* UK: Luniver. .

Xie, J. Z. (2013). A novel bat algorithm based on differential operator and Levy flights trajectory. *Computational Intelligence and Neuroscience.*

Yang, X. S. (2011). Bat algorithm for multi-objective optimisation. *Int. J. Bio-Inspired Computation*, 267-274.

Yang, X. S., Karamanoglu, M., Fong, S. (2012). Bat aglorithm for topology optimization in microelectronic applications. *Conference on Future Generation Communication Technology*, (pp. 150–155).

Yang, X.-S. (2010). A New Metaheuristic Bat-Inspired Algorithm. *Nature Inspired Coop-erative Strategies for Optimization (NISCO 2010)* (pp. 65-74). Springer.

Zadeh, L. A. (1965). Fuzzy sets. *Information and control, 8*(3), 338-353.

www.ingramcontent.com/pod-product-compliance
Lightning Source LLC
Chambersburg PA
CBHW071228050326
40689CB00011B/2497

* 9 7 8 1 5 1 1 4 1 0 5 2 6 *